Cola Bilkuei was born into the Dinka tribal group in the southern Sudan. After an epic journey through Africa, he was granted official UN refugee status and now lives in Australia where he hones his skills as a DJ, as well as actively helping other Sudanese refugees to find shelter and assimilate in Australia.

BOY SOLDIER

cola bilkuei

PAN

Pan Macmillan Australia

First published 2008 in Macmillan by Pan Macmillan Australia Pty Limited
1 Market Street, Sydney
This Pan edition published in 2010
by Pan Macmillan Australia Pty Limited

A CIP Catalogue is available for this title from the
National Library of Australia.

ISBN: 978 0 3304 0377 1

Bilkuei, Cola
Child soldiers—Sudan—Biography.
Refugees—Sudan—Biography.
Refugees—Australia—Biography.
362.87092

Typeset in Granjon by Midland Typesetters, Australia
Printed in Australia by McPherson's Printing Group
Title typeface by Henry Illingworth

Papers used by Pan Macmillan Australia Pty Limited are natural, recyclable products made
from wood grown in sustainable forests. The manufacturing processes conform to the
environmental regulations of the country of origin.

For Father Dominic Baldwin,
Jacob Van Garderen
and
Dennis Biong Mading

Acknowledgements

To MY BROTHER, Monyleck Biem, who started me on my series of adventures good, bad and indifferent. Although these adventures were often dangerous, eventually they led me to the freedom of Australia.

To my mother in heaven, Ajak Arop, who taught me the meaning of love and respect. I thank you for instilling confidence in me – without that confidence my struggle too would have been lost.

To my father Biem Ngor Bilkuei, who looked after me when I was young despite his own scars and torments.

Also to my elder sister in heaven, Ajok Biem and my baby sister in heaven, Athien Biem.

To my elder brother in heaven, Mijok Biem and my little brother in heaven, Thonager Biem.

To all my Pan–Bilkuei family for their unity and respect of history and keeping the family spirit alive.

To Philip Ross: we started this project, and my special thanks goes to you for your good heart. I think I owe you a million dollars. Without your support this book may have not been possible. Special thanks to the Blacktown Migrant Resources Centre for all your help.

To Malcolm Knox: you are a wonderful, loving person on the Earth! You are the person who opened the way forward for this piece of work. I know there are millions of people out there who have similar stories, but it was through God's work that I was given your email address by good Samaritan Dr Ralph Sawyer at a private function in Sydney. You have continued to feed me and accommodate me during the time of our writing together. Of course I also thank your lovely wife Wenona, and your kids Callum and Lilian; you have all welcomed and supported me and shown me love from the drafting to the finishing of this book.

Anthony – you are the best friend I have ever made.

To Tony Chappel and family – thanks for your great help. You did countless things for me, like paying school fees, pocket money and tours. You are a great guy and a leader, who always looks after people from disadvantaged backgrounds, no matter their race.

Karen Du Plessis and your kids Simon and Lukas; Irma Du Plessis; Andriaes Benzuihout; Sophie Marrie; Deon Garderen; and Sarin Garderen.

Dr Francios Deng and Dorothy Deng; Daniel Jok Deng; Steven Boakye; Max Lucas; Mavis Smith; Lt General Oyei Deng Ajak; Uncle Louis Mayar Bilkuei; Chief Seji Makuei; Chief Deng Mayar Bilkuei; Uncle Chol Bilkuei; Uncle Panom Cothcoth; Uncle Majak Dau; Uncle Deng Maker Bilkuei; Mabek Lang, the Panaruu Commissioner.

Beny Wian, our community spiritual leader in Baal Sudan; Dr BM Benjamin; Dr Mark Awouro; Uncle Ajang Chiman; Uncle Deng Ngor; and Dr William Biong Deng Kwol Mading Deng.

To Mr Dermot Donnors, the senior Veritas Principal, the teachers and lovely staff, and students who showed me and Bol Bol a great love. Your teachings gave me a great motivation that has really kept me going.

To Terry Hick, in Johannesburg – you were my boss, who employed me in a country where millions and millions of people go searching for jobs every morning. Today I find it easier to interact with other employees at my workplace and have respect for team leaders, managers and directors, thanks to you.

Williams Agar; DJ Victor Lopez; Antony Lopez; DJ Samrai; DJ Demize; J Smoove; Charles; Melissa Uttley; Tha Mic; F2 and C2; and Eyob Yesus from Luscious Entertainment.

Mr Zux from Big One Productions, my best friend on the music side for a long time; you are a great man with great studio skills, one of the best African rappers, a DJ and producer, putting your full force into helping African youths to record their music. Your vision to help these kids stay away from crime and keep them busy with the microphone is indeed a great help to their families personally, and to the safety of the community.

Bilkuei Productions and its staff work hard to support our artist Hot Dogg throughout his involvement with the Darfurian non-governmental organisation in Winnipeg, Canada to raise funds for Darfurian children in Sudan.

Bonabas Deng Yel; Todd Williams from Merrylands Youth Centre; and Mijok Lang aka Hot Dogg.

Mayoum Mijok and family for your support throughout my process of coming to Australia, the promised land. And to your lovely wife, Martha, whom I to used to wake up sometimes at 2 am or 3 am when I called from Africa. I now know how getting the time right is so important in the Western world!

Plath Miaker; the Nyok Dau family; Monyjok Bogout; Sister Louise, director of JRS Pretoria; Jing Thomas; Benjamin Bol Bol; Angelo Kuot Garang; Charles Akuei; Cirelo Cier Jel; Jackson Mijok; Atok Dan; Thomas Wour; Mayak Seji; Emmanuel Hubbi; Kabelo; Ryan Bowers; Martina Mthembu; and Ronnie Vyslouzel.

Russell Beaten; Santino Aher; Peter Deng; James Makur Mijok; Atak Deng Akol; Biar Deng Dut; Daniel Magot; David Poundak; Ring Kolang; Martin Kadit; Ayak Makueth; and Malual Madut.

G Rida, Olivier Strobel, Alice Deady, Major General Michael Char, Rev Joseph Ayok, Afrocent, Tera, M Phasasi, Machodi, Alex Llavero, George Giannopoulos, Dr Angok Kuol, Atok Majok, Alang Majok, Chief Miaker Dau, Chief Malual Miyniel, Bul Miyoum, Bith Are, Danny Beaten and the Beaten Family, James Tut, MD Andrea, Dre Chol, Akol Kiir, Chan Dut Kon, Ali Garang, Dut Yaak Dut, Mayak Seji, Ajang Jok Ajang, Akim Majak, Anyuop Majak, Tabau Dau, Christina Adau Miaker, Pual Miyoum, Mr Tong Jel, Garang Yaak, Arakangelo Nyuol Madut, Phillip Tole, Sr Gemma, Sr Anita, Sr Sophia, Sr Rita, Mr Angelo Diing, Lam Buot.

To all my colleagues who were in Zimbabwe.

And to all my new friends whom I made in Australia who have shown a great love in me as a person, I deeply thank each individual.

Contents

Cola's Journey

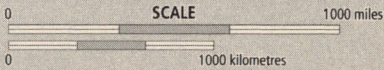

SCALE

0   1000 miles

0   1000 kilometres

First Light

Near dawn, when all is still, my ancestors come to me. They bring me the taste of the land: ripe new corn stalks against the dampness of the River Nile; the sound of crackling fire; the scent of cattle and the fresh milk that filled my belly every morning. Most of all they bring the feeling of safety that came from my mother's warm embrace. As I close my eyes, the sounds of fire are layered with the sounds of singing and drums beating to rhythms that I have not heard since I left my homeland.

I left when I was a child.

My land was rich, maybe not in a Western sense, but rich in history. My people weren't just connected with their culture, they lived it . . . and then there was war. The land, the people and the history are all still there, but now I open my eyes to a new world. As a refugee I have my memories and it's up to me and me alone to create a future in which those memories are not lost. I also realise that my new life is just that – a new life that will bring its own memories, experiences and challenges. I've had many journeys in my short life and yet I know that I have many more to face before I'm through.

My great-grandfather on my father's side was called Bilkuei. He had forty-seven children and eight wives.

My grandfather was Ngor Bilkuei. He had four wives and fifteen children.

My father, Biem Ngor, was the firstborn of Ngor Bilkuei and the only child of his first wife. My father had two wives. My mother, Ajak Arop, was his first wife and I was the fifth child of seven. My father's second wife, my stepmother, had five children.

I pray for one wife and as many children as can be safe under my protection.

Chapter I

Sudan

I was born Chol Biem Ngor Bilkuei. My friends call me Cola, a name I gave myself in 1999. I don't know how old I am, as I don't know when my birthday is. I grew up in a village called Baal in the area of Panaruu in southern Sudan. My people are known as the Dinka, but we are divided into many sub-tribes. Ours, the Panaruu sub-tribe, centring on Baal and a cluster of neighbouring villages, was about 96,000 in number. Our larger tribe is known by different names: we are called the Ruweng, the Ngok, and the Padang people, depending on which of the surrounding tribes you are talking to. The biggest town in our area was called Panrieng, which had about 10,000 inhabitants. My great-grandfather was the chief of this sub-tribe, so my family was important. I grew up surrounded by my parents, brothers and sisters and the 2000 cattle we owned, and beyond that by our greater Bilkuei family and the thousands of people in our Panaruu community.

When I think about my village and all that my life consisted of, it feels as though I'm looking back at someone else's life. My new life in Sydney, Australia, is a world away from everything I knew back home.

My father, Biem Ngor Bilkuei, tried his best to protect us from a world that he saw as dangerous. People called him 'Biem-*dit*', which is a sign of respect, like calling a man 'sir'. To him, the world outside our village offered more threat than opportunity. Up until the age of about eight, I never ventured more than a few kilometres outside our village. I never saw a white person. There were no roads going through our village, only dirt paths and open spaces where people walked. On the rare occasions that I ever saw or heard motor vehicles, they scared me. At night we could see the lights of lorries passing on a distant highway, but we couldn't see the trucks themselves. All we saw were their beams in the dusty night air, accompanied by the faraway roar of their engines.

Once we heard a helicopter and saw it in the distance. I also remember when we were told the Concorde was flying over us. We lay on the ground and watched the white contrail cross the sky. Someone got it into their head that these aeroplanes were driven by white ladies, and they'd cry out, 'There goes the white lady's aeroplane!' My mother said these planes stole children to take them to America, wherever that was.

I didn't go to school, so everything I knew I learnt from the people in the village and from my own experience as a herd boy working with my family. My earliest memories of childhood are of time spent with my father working the cattle on land that was shared by our community. My great-grandfather Bilkuei was the clan chief until he died in 1935, and then the title was passed to one of my grandfather's brothers, Makuei Bilkuei. He was the ultimate judge of disputes and the head organiser. Below him were the elders, who attained their position when they reached a certain age, and together solved problems in the chief's name. Ranks were determined by generational groups: once your generation came of age, you were marked with knife cuts horizontally across your forehead. The bigger your forehead, the more room for these marks! But they meant you were respected.

The land we lived on was flat and bare, except for one tremendous tree close to our main hut, which grew many metres high and spread much shade under its wide branches. But despite the heat of the sun, none of us used the tree for shade. It was a sacred place, where we would only go to show respect to our ancestors. Grass grew high around the tree and it was full of snakes. It was at the tree that we would make sacrifices. On special occasions – if it had been very dry and we needed rain, for example, or if an important person was sick – someone would cut the grass and kill or carry the snakes away (Dinka weren't allowed to kill some snakes, such as pythons, because they were sacred), and the tree would provide a place from which the elders would sacrifice a cow. Normally we didn't kill and butcher cattle for food. They were too vital for that. We kids would look forward to these sacrifice ceremonies because they meant we would eat well. While the adults ate the flesh of the cattle, the intestines and organs would be cooked for the children. An elder would gather up our share and feign throwing it one way, then the other, and then throw it up in handfuls; we would fall over ourselves trying to get to it.

Also on these occasions, after we had eaten, the elders in my family would tell stories. These stories would include histories of people in the village and of wars between tribes. Here was where I heard that my grandfather and his twin brother were killed on the same day, before I was born, when they were among a large group of local chiefs and elders who were called to a meeting by Arabs from northern Sudan and then massacred.

The tree stood like a museum, with bones from different sacrifices left around its trunk. When there was a harvest, some maize would be scattered around the base of the tree before anyone ate. A trench, like a moat, about four metres wide and one metre deep, separated the sacred area from the area we were allowed to use, and this was a boundary we all respected. If we wandered too close, elders would call us away. In the rainy season, we didn't want to go there anyway, as bats hung in the branches and dangerous animals – even lions – might lurk in the long grass. I remember believing that if I went near the tree, terrible things, like sickness or bad luck for my family, would follow.

My grandmother, who was blind, would often be found sitting near the tree, but only on the outside of the trench. It seemed to us as if she and the tree had become one. Neither of them could see, both were weathered by age, and both represented the heart of our village. All the villagers recognised my grandmother's spiritual powers, as she was seen to carry within her the spirits of our ancestors. At ceremonies, such as weddings and funerals, or when someone was sick, she was brought in as an embodiment of the ancestors to raise her hands and bring down their blessings.

I never remember seeing many manufactured items in my village: no steel, no plastic, nothing like a bicycle or even a tin can. Apart from some metal items such as razor blades, knife blades and the zinc sheeting used in some buildings, everything we had was made from the environment around us. Buckets were woven from wood. When the rainy season stopped, the people in the village would dig wells up to thirty metres deep with sharpened hoes and spears. If they didn't find water, they just kept digging. A good well would become permanent. In the rainy season, yards and houses would be built, and the excavated holes would make new wells. The drier it was, the further we had to travel to a well with drinkable water. The River Nile was four hours' walk away.

The members of the Bilkuei clan in Baal lived in a compound of about ten huts. The two largest were for cattle, housing about fifty cows each. If a cow was sick, it would be brought in alone until it was better. Our immediate family had two smaller huts, which consisted of mud walls with grass roofs and hard dirt floors. They had no internal walls or partitions. They were simple, but they did what they were built for. One of them had a large hole in the ground which my mother would use for cooking.

My mother smoked an African pipe, but never in front of my father, so this hut also provided her with a place to hide her habit. There was nothing complicated about my father's prohibition: he didn't smoke and didn't like the smell of it. He thought smoke would contaminate the milking of the cows or the cooking. Nor did he like the smell of it on her breath. In other families women could smoke, but not in ours. The smell of the fire masked the smell of her pipe. She knew she was safe because my father never went near the cooking hut until the meal was ready to eat, which always took place outside. A typical meal was maize pap, ground and mashed with water – the nearest Australian food I can think of is mashed potatoes. At other times the maize would be prepared and baked into tiny balls, like couscous. If there was no maize we drank milk. Milk, milk, milk, every day. Today, as an adult, I don't like milk at all.

Before my father married his second wife, which happened when I was about six, my parents would sleep in the other hut. Mostly we kids slept in the cows' hut, unless the weather was really bad – and even then my parents didn't like to share their hut with us!

My father was a hard worker and probably appreciated what little space was his by nightfall. Actually, when I think about it, it wasn't that he was a hard worker; in fact he was probably lazy. He didn't have a set role in the village, like a hunter or a builder, although he was often appointed to go to other villages and buy cattle.

For some seasons when I was a child, my father lived in the city of Bentiu, the capital of Unity State, or al-Wahda. Bentiu, seven hundred and fifty kilometres south-west of Khartoum, was two or three days' walk from our village, and had a lot of oilfields around it. My father worked there as a wildlife officer for the government. When he came back to the village, rather than work, he preferred to boss others around and point out the shortcomings of those who were actually doing the work.

He liked everyone to think he was a hard worker; he was the sort of man who boasted a lot, and if you didn't know him you would be forgiven for thinking he was the toughest, hardest working person in the village. Truthfully, that title would have been shared between my uncles and the younger members of my family, including my mother, my brothers and sisters, and my cousins – everyone in the family, in fact, except my father! But he made sure his reputation for industry spread far and wide. That was one thing he definitely worked hard at.

I had four brothers and two sisters. One of my brothers died as a baby – I was too young to know what was going on and don't really remember anything about it. The eldest of us all was my sister Ajok, followed by my brother Mijok, my brother Monyleck, the baby who died, then me, my younger brother Thonager and the baby of our family, my sister Athien.

During the day my father's four brothers and my own elder brothers would look after the large cattle and I was given the calves. I was small for my age so it made sense that I looked after the smallest of the cattle. But there were a lot of them – up to two or three hundred. First thing in the morning I would be given the job of cleaning up after the cows, picking up their dung and mess once they had been milked. This usually resulted in me getting covered from head to toe in cow dung.

It was bad enough most days, but unmentionable if the cows suffered from diarrhoea the night before! Every day Thonager and I would collect the dung and put it out in the sun to dry. It was then used as fuel for the fires we lit every afternoon around 4 pm to keep the cows warm and to ward off mosquitoes. Sometimes these fires were so dense it would seem as though the whole village was burning down. My childhood memories are saturated with the smell of cow dung, whether it was fresh or burning.

Nothing was ever wasted in our village. After the dung had been burnt, the ash was used. We smeared our bodies with it. This was not so much for decoration as to show that we were men with a real job: to protect the cattle. Without the painted-on ash we would be considered too clean, too lazy and too much of a target for teasing by men and older boys, who would say that if we were too clean we looked like girls. It wasn't just for show, though. In Dinka culture it is of prime importance to protect your cattle – if you looked like someone who didn't work and get dirty, you might be placing your cows in danger of being stolen.

We also used the ash in our hair. Mixed with cow urine, it created a soft paste that would sit on the surface of our hair, lasting up to two weeks. When it was washed out it would leave our hair lighter coloured and straighter, which we liked for celebrations. I think it also made our hair grow faster! Hair was one of the few things we had to compete over. Our mothers would cut it with old blades and create circles and patterns of hair which we, as kids, thought were very fashionable.

Late in the morning I would milk the cows with my brothers, Mijok and Monyleck. As soon as Thonager was old enough, he helped out as well. It was important to keep the calves away from their mothers, to prevent them from suckling and using up all the milk. Milking was done by hand into thirty or forty dried gourds. Without any refrigeration, milk couldn't be kept, so every family had its own cows and its own milk. Nobody bought or sold milk – because everybody had it! Milk was one thing there was never any lack of.

When we finished milking we would sit together as a family and drink the fresh milk. The rest of my day would be filled with looking after the calves, while Thonager tagged along, doing what he could.

If a cow was having trouble producing enough milk, or if her calf had died, we needed to help the cow along. The best way of doing this was for someone to place their mouth over the cow's vagina and blow into it, while rubbing the teat. You would do this until you felt the teat fill with milk. The worst part was that sometimes when you blew into the cow, the cow returned the favour by kicking you or, even worse, filling your mouth with urine. You soon learnt when to turn your head!

Our cows were the centre of our universe. Sometimes I thought they were given more importance than the people in our village. The cattle were always treated with respect and when our village got together at night to sing, more often than not we sang about our cattle. The songs would tell of how strong the bulls were or how beautiful the cows were and how they were admired for helping to keep our village alive.

Everyone else would make up songs about their cattle to sing at our night-time gatherings, but I was always frustrated because I could never come up with a song about mine. As a child I was very shy and found it hard to perform in front of what seemed to be such a big crowd. There was too much at stake. If you couldn't sing well, you were mocked – you would not get a wife, you would not be important or successful, you were not a real man. I loved my cattle and wished I could honour them as everyone else did, but I got too nervous to think. I still get nervous in front of groups, even if I know the people. But nothing is as scary to me as trying to think up a song about my cattle in front of my village.

With so many cattle to look after, my father decided that there needed to be a way of dividing up who would inherit them when we became adults. His solution was simple – they would be divided by colour. The black and white cattle would go to Mijok, red to Monyleck, I got the motley ones, and so on. It may not have been an even distribution but we were happy with the idea of it. In any case, the distribution never happened: the Arab militias sent by the government in Khartoum were to come and take most of our cattle away.

I spent a lot of time in the bush near our village, playing with Thonager and other children who had similar jobs to mine. During the dry season – October to April – the flat open ground where the cows grazed was very dusty. But after it started raining in May, the grass grew long and low scrubby bushes would spring up. We would play with mud, using it to build models of houses, cattle and other animals, and people. Our mud people would resemble real people that we either liked or disliked. The ones that we disliked would be destroyed in our mud world and given a mud funeral.

Most of the time I was well behaved, but I was often in trouble for staying out too late with the cattle. I would venture so far into my imaginary mud worlds that I would lose track of time altogether and not return with the calves until it was almost dark. If you lost track of time, or worse still lost track of your cattle, you could be beaten to within an inch of your life. Many things could go wrong if you didn't pay attention to your cattle. They could stray onto agricultural land and destroy crops; they could be stolen; or they could be attacked by lions or hyenas. If any of these things happened, a beating was sure to follow.

If I was beaten too often by someone (such as one of my father's many half-brothers), they would end up having a 'mud funeral' and I would risk repeating the whole process by getting carried away with my revenge.

We often played sport together, sometimes for fun, but sometimes as important preparation. The main games involved fighting with spears made from cane and shields from cowskin or goatskin. These were not real weapons, but we soon learned to imitate the way they were used by adults – and for that matter children – in times of war or tribal dispute. My father would make my brothers and me fight against each other, so that he could see what skills we had developed. I was best at stick fighting, whereas Mijok and Monyleck were good at wrestling and throwing spears.

I was always amazed watching Mijok and Monyleck fighting each other. They were so different from one another; Mijok was quiet and gentle, while Monyleck was naturally belligerent and always seemed on the defensive.

He had a lot to be defensive about. Monyleck had trouble fitting in with the rest of the family. He was the only one who had been given the opportunity to go to secondary school and the only one to really experience the outside world. Before I was born, my father would take Monyleck to the town with him. Mijok, as the eldest, had important duties back in the village. As second-born, Monyleck was lucky. Our father had decided that he could be educated and become the brains of the family. He started school in Bentiu, and later went to a school in Khartoum. None of the rest of us went to Khartoum, and I still haven't ever been there. He would come back with stories of how big it was, how many buildings and cars he had seen. Most Dinka avoided Khartoum, though. It was the capital of our country, but it was also the city of the northern people who had done so much to threaten the Dinka south. Some Dinka who went to Khartoum were recruited into the government army and posted to the south; this was another reason for the men we knew to steer clear of the place.

At this time there was peace between the north and the south, but our father had once been a fighter. What he told us about the war, from my earliest childhood, was basic but still accurate. The people in the north, who controlled the government, were Muslim Arabs. We in the south were black Africans and our religion was a mixture of Christian and tribal beliefs. The northerners wanted our land, our cattle, our water, and finally our oil, and they came to steal it from us. We in the south had to form an army to resist their attacks. This was a rudimentary way of telling the story, but like I said, it was the truth.

School had changed Monyleck, so that when he came back he was different from the rest of us. He thought our father wasn't looking after us very well, and was neglecting our mother now he had married his second wife, so Monyleck was in a hurry to become independent and lead the family. He always had an independent streak and he often clashed with our father. Twice when he was at school, men from the United Nations had offered to resettle Monyleck elsewhere – in Kenya and the United States of America. Monyleck saw it as an opportunity to further his education and help the family. But our father refused.

When he was at school, Monyleck suffered because he had fewer clothes than the other students. His shoes wore out because our father didn't have enough money for new ones. Yet when he came back to the village, Monyleck wore his school uniform in open defiance of the elders, who tried to convince him that he was insulting the other members of the family. We other boys went around naked, and even the elders only wore a loincloth, yet Monyleck was dressed like a king. But he refused to obey. He was proud of his clothes. The elders beat him to put him in his place.

They didn't think much of education. I sympathised with him. We smaller kids sometimes got the chance to try his clothes on, and if they'd been ours, we'd have worn them all the time as well. He looked as though he belonged to a different culture, a different place, and as his little brother I was in awe of this.

One time, Monyleck brought a leather soccer ball and a whistle back from school. He organised a game of football, but he was the only one with shoes and when the rest of us kicked the ball it hurt our toes. He would blow his whistle and laugh at us and tell us to keep playing. Easy for him to say: he was the only one whose feet were not aching!

It wasn't just the clothes that set Monyleck apart. After he came back from school, he didn't like to look after the cows because he thought it was beneath him and he started to think that some of our customs were dated. He said that using the ash left over from burnt cow dung to cover our bodies was strange, and mocked us for doing it.

Sometimes I was envious of Monyleck. I could see what a hard time he had, but I wanted to know what he knew and I wanted to see the things he had seen. Even though his experience was so different from mine, I secretly hoped to follow in his footsteps. I dreamed about running away to Khartoum. There had to be a better life than humiliating myself trying to think up songs about my cattle! Under his influence, I started to wonder if our customs were strange. I'd never thought so before – I thought everyone did as we did. But now I began wanting to be like him, to learn about other worlds and to have a life that didn't involve blowing into cows' vaginas. I started talking about life outside our village, making up wild fantasies about what people did and where I was going to go. Whenever I did, my mother would bring me back to reality by reminding me of the chores I should have been doing.

***

My mother was a quiet lady. She was thin and of medium height for a Dinka woman. She plaited her hair, and sometimes tied a green cloth around it. She was honest and a good judge of character. A good-looking woman, she smiled a lot and liked to keep the peace between her husband and her sons by making light of things. She didn't intervene forcefully, though, and at times I thought she was too quiet. There were times where I would be beaten by an uncle or someone else in the community for neglecting my calves, and my mother could never seem to muster up the courage to say anything. She would ask why I had been beaten. When I explained, she always seemed to take the adults' side regardless of whether or not I was innocent. If someone complained to her about me, she would instantly believe them and give me a beating as punishment.

I don't think she was trying to be mean; she just wanted us to show respect and be respected by those in the village. My mother was strict about following the rules of our culture, which are very traditional and *very* different from the rules that I now see around me in Australia.

In Dinka culture, if the children show a lack of respect, the people in the community look first at what the parents are doing wrong. It was important to my parents that the whole family had a good reputation. If I was considered a bad child, the community would judge my brothers and sisters by my behaviour. A bad reputation was like a disease – it was contagious and hard to shake. It could affect everything from how you were treated to who you were allowed to marry later in life. Also, my parents believed that if I showed disrespect to someone, that person – even if they were not a member of the family – had a right to discipline me, including hitting me to teach me a lesson. I was not just a child of one family – I was a child of the community.

Looking back, I wish I could have spent more time alone with my mother. But I was always busy, and she was always busy, and it would have been frowned upon for a boy to be too dependent on his mother. I wish it could have been otherwise.

Throughout the night, even though my brothers and I could sleep around the fires we had lit in the afternoon, we still had to make sure the cows were safe and watch for intruders. The largest cows were put on the outside of a big circle, with the calves and my brothers and me in the middle. This was to protect us from lions, hyenas and any humans that decided to come our way. The big cows knew where to stand, and they were tethered to coloured stakes we had driven into the ground. They weren't afraid of any other animals, so at night-time they protected us. We also had spears and sticks. It might not sound like it, but it was a restful way to sleep. Maybe we were so tired from working and playing all day, we had no energy left to be scared.

In the rainy season the grass around the village would grow long, high above our heads, and wild animals such as lions and hyenas would venture onto our land. I remember one night a hyena came and killed three of our goats. My uncles heard the goats screaming and started to wake everyone up. We were always taught to make as much noise as possible if we were attacked, both to alert everyone else and to scare the predator. Now my uncles were screaming, 'Hyenas, hyenas, hyenas!' Everyone woke up to see the hyena running off into the distance. We went to check on the goats. Out of the thirty or so goats we had in our herd, one was missing, two were dead and one was half-eaten.

Everyone stayed awake until morning. We knew the hyena would return. Lions usually took their prey away with them, or attacked and didn't return. Hyenas were different.

In the morning, the older members of the family followed the hyena's footprints. They knew he wouldn't have gone far on a full stomach, and he'd been dragging a goat with him. Eventually they found him sleeping, and attacked him with their spears until he was dead. They came back celebrating, with the hyena carcass held high in the air. Hyena meat and juice was said to be good for pain relief, so some of the family would use it for medicinal purposes, and its skin would be used as a rug. If there was one rule that applied to the whole of our life, it was that nothing went to waste.

Even though my father was a wealthy man with a lot of livestock, life was never easy for my family. My father was a strict disciplinarian; he had lived through many years of war, witnessing all kinds of atrocities. In a way I think he was so strict with us as a way of preparing us for our own manhood, our own conflicts, our own wars.

Even when we were very young he would tell us that no man is born at the same time as his father, therefore no man should rely on his father to be there until the day he dies. He taught us to rely on ourselves alone.

My father taught me many things about the war. At nighttime, he loved to have a drink and call us around the fire to tell us stories about his past. He told us how Sudan had gained independence in 1956, after the British colonists left, when he was a very young man. We had no idea what 1956 meant or what white people looked like or where they came from, so our father educated us by telling us about the British and their colonial wars. He said that within a year of independence, fighting broke out between separatist southern rebels – Anyanya ('snake poison') – and the government officials from the north. The British had kept us and the Muslims separated, but after independence we were lumped together within one country. He said the reason for the fighting was that the Dinka had the best land, water, oil and cattle, and the Arabs from the north wanted to take it from us. They also wanted to steal us for slaves, we were told. Most of what I knew of Arabs came from my father, though I do remember some Arab traders coming to the village to exchange salt, sugar and tea for our maize, sorghum, goats or cattle.

Our family did have some links further back with the Arabs. My great-grandfather Bilkuei and his brother and sister were taken as children to be slaves in northern Sudan, and then in Egypt. As an adult he came back to Khartoum and became a Muslim. His owner, an old lady, was happy with the way he worked, so she gave him one of her daughters as a concubine. (He still has some descendants in Khartoum.) But then he was visited by his ancestors' spirits, who called him back to the south. When he returned to his Dinka home, people were entranced by his experience and his spiritual powers. He cured people and animals of disease, and was given cattle, wives and land. This was how our sub-tribe had been formed – in some part thanks to his life among the Arabs. But that was long ago now.

My father had joined the Anyanya in 1955 and fought with them, on and off, until 1972 when a peace agreement was reached and signed in Addis Ababa, the capital city of Ethiopia. Over the next eleven years of peace he divided his time between working outside the village as a wildlife officer for the government and working the cattle with the family. Ajok, Mijok and Monyleck were born towards the end of the war, then came the baby who died. I think I was born between 1976 and 1978. After me was Thonager, and finally Athien who was born around 1981. I remember being offered my baby brother and sister to hold, but I was too scared of dropping them and ran away.

In 1983 Arab militias started to appear in the villages, carrying guns and riding in on camels and donkeys. The militias were unofficial bands of Muslim fighters who did not wear government army uniforms but were armed and paid by Khartoum. They were to do the government's dirty work while the rulers could pretend to look the other way. At gunpoint they stole cattle and children. The peace between the north and south was breaking down again, and soon another civil war broke out, with the SPLA (Sudan People's Liberation Army – the military wing) and SPLM (Sudan People's Liberation Movement – the political wing) on one side and the government army and the militias they supported on the other. The militias would come in first to terrorise the people, and then the government soldiers would follow up to take over and establish control.

The SPLA was founded by a Dinka leader, John Garang, following an internal struggle in the Anyanya. The Anyanya had splintered already, since 1972, between those who accepted the peace and those (the Anyanya II) who had wanted to maintain the fight between 1972 and 1983. The movement Garang founded in 1983 was more of a student movement, made up of younger people, who took over the Anyanya's bases in Ethiopia.

This time my father and my two elder brothers, Monyleck and Mijok, joined the SPLA and went to war. My father went first in 1983 but fought close to home, so he would often return for a couple of days after stints of three or four months. He didn't talk about what had happened, telling us we were too young to be asking questions. I have to confess that we weren't too scared for him when he was gone. Things were more relaxed and we had more freedom without him. But of course we celebrated when he came home too.

Mijok joined the SPLA in early 1983, Monyleck in 1984. Both were sent to Ethiopia for training. The Ethiopian government, which was antagonistic to Khartoum, had long given sanctuary to the Anyanya, and then, when John Garang formed the SPLA, his new army was able to take over these bases over the border. Ethiopia was a communist state backed by Russia and Cuba, but supported rebel movements throughout Africa more to spread its power than to advance its ideology. The driving force of the SPLA was always to defend southern Sudan against the incursions of the government, not to set up a communist state.

My brothers would be gone for two years, and we would never hear either of them speak a word about what they had been through or how they had been trained. It was as if those two years didn't exist for them.

While they were away, life at home continued more or less as usual, except that we all had to work harder to fill the gap left by my brothers. My sister Ajok would look after more of the cattle, as would Thonager and I. The baby of our family, Athien, was still too young to know what was going on. She spent most of her time helping our blind grandmother, my father's mother, around the village. Athien became her eyes, describing everything she saw and leading my grandmother everywhere she wanted to go. Everyone loved Athien – she was beautiful, kind and, perhaps because of her constant attachment to my grandmother, she seemed like an old soul.

Ajok, being the eldest, took on what she saw as our father's role – disciplining us children. I don't think I'd ever been slapped so many times in my life! Ajok and I had never been very close, and her assuming my father's role during that time didn't do anything to improve our relationship.

Over the next few months it was obvious that the fighting was getting closer and closer to our village. We were now hearing gunshots in the distance on a daily basis. Mainly we'd hear them in the morning, when they would pierce the quiet air. With my big brothers and our father gone, the time had come to make a decision on whether we should stay or go. My mother decided we should leave.

Our family fled to what we assumed would be a place of safety on the banks of the Nile, three days' walking to the north-east. There the trees grew thickly by the river and offered hiding places. We packed up as much as we could carry – some water and blankets – and left our village behind. Some of my uncles stayed to protect and look after the cattle and, if need be, defend our village. It was hard for us to leave because we knew that in other villages the militias and government officials had looted everything, burning down homes and destroying crops. They killed people, took many women and children for slaves, and stole the livestock to take to farms further north or to eat immediately. We didn't know what we would return to – or if we would return at all.

We walked for days, Athien guiding my grandmother with every step. It was strange for me at first because, as a boy in Dinka culture, as soon as you're old enough to run you're taught not to stay by your mother's side. Even though I saw my mother every day, I was never as physically close to her as my sisters had been. While we walked towards the Nile, however, we all needed to stay close in order to survive. At the age of about eight, as I was then, I found that I liked being close to my mother. She was fairly thin, and very quiet, content to keep her own counsel. While we were walking, I felt like nothing significant could have changed because she was there. The village might have been burnt down, but my mother was my home. It didn't matter about what had happened to the huts, as long as I was with her.

Once we reached the Nile, for some of the time it felt as though we were on a family holiday. There were no cows to look after and what food we ate now came from the river. I didn't know how to swim, having had only wet-season ponds around the village, and so I would stand on the bank with fishing lines and hooks. We would fish and eat the grasses that grew along the banks and in the river itself. As I was the oldest boy, I felt like the man of the family, making sure we all had enough to eat and that everyone was happy.

This area of the Nile was narrow and dotted with small islands on which people had built shacks. We clustered on the banks with seven families from our sub-tribe who had all come to this place. Everything was green and the Nile smelt like fresh rain. It was different from our village, not just the landscape but the sense of living from the river. It was like a new way of life and, despite the fact that we were fleeing from war, it felt relaxed. It was a life I thought I could get used to easily.

But all too soon our new life was interrupted, as the sound of machine-gun fire returned suddenly one early morning. It grew louder and louder – the fighting was coming our way. In a panic we all ran, dropping everything where it was. We were in such a frightened rush we had forgotten that my grand-mother couldn't run. I stopped and offered to put her on my back but I was too small. My mother pleaded with her to at least try to run, grabbing her hand, leading her through the bush. It was impossible. Eventually my grandmother stopped. Resigned to being left behind, she told us to go. The gunfire was approaching closer and closer, and we could now hear soldiers' voices coming in our direction. We were sure they were government troops. Without saying as much, my grand-mother was offering us a clear choice: we could either stay with her and all be killed, or leave her there and hope the soldiers wouldn't pass her way.

We left her. We tried the best we could to hide her in the tall grass so that she wouldn't be seen. We cut some more grass and laid it on top of her.

The sun was beating down and we had left in such a hurry that we hadn't brought any water. If the soldiers didn't get her, we feared the heat would. With the sound of gunfire almost upon us, we prayed for her and ran.

I can't remember how long we ran for, but I do remember the guilt of having left a defenceless blind woman to die. We all felt it desperately. She was my father's mother. How could we explain to him what had happened and why we had left her there?

But there was no time to think of that. We were running for our own lives, and when you are doing that you think of nothing but survival. Eventually we found a safe place to hide among some trees. We waited for the soldiers to pass, all of us anxious about what had happened to my grandmother. As day fell to night the fighting continued in the distance, but it wouldn't be safe for us to check on my grandmother until the following day.

My mother shook with fear as she tried to keep us all quiet in the dark. My uncle, Duop Mayer, and his family were with us, and as things calmed down he wanted to light a fire and smoke his pipe. Some of the others warned him not to, but he (and my mother) loved to smoke and couldn't be dissuaded.

We dozed, but were woken suddenly by gunfire very close to us. Frightened for our lives, we all ran in different directions. Duop's son, my cousin Ajit, was Thonager's age. He was left behind. I remember him crying out to me, 'Chol! Chol!', but I ran, as did everyone else.

Some hours after everybody scattered into the bush, when the gunfire had gone away, we eventually converged. I came across one of my aunties and her son, who were also running. Together we kept walking all night.

By daybreak I was exhausted. The fighting had stopped, or at least I couldn't hear any gunshots. We met my mother and Athien, and we decided to go back to the Nile. It wasn't easy to retrace our steps because we'd run through thick bush, but in the afternoon we stumbled across the place where we had left my grandmother. She was lying, quite still, in the grass. My mother screamed out to her and to our surprise she moved – she was alive! Apart from being thirsty and scared, she was all right. The soldiers had fought all around her, never noticing that she was tucked into the bush. Athien, as if nothing had happened, took our grandmother by the hand and led her out of her hiding spot.

That night there was a big argument about what had happened to Ajit in all the confusion. His father, Duop, said Ajit had been shot dead while he was carrying him. But others said they had heard Ajit calling out later. We weren't to find out for many years what had happened to the little boy, but it is a story worth telling. He was captured by the Arabs and taken as a slave to the north. There he grew up and, as an Arabic-speaking Dinka man, he joined the Sudanese army and was posted to the south. He fell in love with a girl, and when he was considering proposing to her she asked him some questions about his family. It turned out that she and he were first cousins! That put paid to the marriage (we have the same incest taboo as Western culture) but it led to a family reunion. Ajit met his mother and father again, and the whole family celebrated to have found him. Nobody talks about the story Duop told, about Ajit being shot.

Days later we returned to our village, not knowing what we would find. As we drew closer we could see smoke rising from where our village stood. When we arrived, we could barely say a word: the government soldiers had burnt it to the ground. Some of my friends had disappeared, either dead or stolen as slaves. Defeated and shocked, we searched for what was left of our huts. Cattle were missing or dead; our maize had been taken, and almost everything else was gone. My uncles who had stayed had fled just in time to avoid being killed and were, like us, returning to see the devastation. We didn't have much apart from our cattle, but it was the only home we'd ever known. To see it destroyed, destroyed a part of us too.

Our family began rebuilding the village straightaway. New mud-and-grass huts were erected, new crops sown. We worked harder than ever to reclaim what was ours.

Soon my father returned home. It wasn't long before he found out what had happened with my grandmother. He wasted no time in showing my mother exactly how he felt. He beat her until she fell to the ground, not in private but in front of the entire village. Their relationship was never to be the same again.

With the village rebuilt and life returning to some semblance of normality, we finally had some good news. It was now around 1985 and Mijok was given leave to return home for two weeks. In the two years he'd been gone he'd spent most of his time in training and hadn't yet fought in the war. The day he came home, our entire village celebrated. Everyone was happy to see him. There was a lot of singing and dancing. A goat was killed, and we ate until our stomachs hurt. Apart from anything else, I think everyone was just happy to be happy.

But his return, and everyone's joy, was short-lived. No sooner had Mijok arrived than a message came that the rest of his group were about to start their first mission in a town to the south. Bam was a government-held town, where the Arabs had taken cattle they had stolen. Mijok had been waiting for his chance to fight, to put into practice what the SPLA had taught him. It seemed strange when he had always been so gentle and peaceful that here he was, eager to fight. He was so impatient to leave that he barely said goodbye. He wasn't about to miss the first battle with his new battalion; he wanted to return a hero, not stay behind on holiday while his friends risked their lives.

My mother was concerned that he wouldn't be safe. Despite his training, Mijok still seemed vulnerable. As a compromise, one of my uncles, Duor Niang, was sent to look out for him. Duor Niang was a civilian but knew how to look after himself. If anyone could look out for Mijok it would be Duor.

Days and weeks passed with no news. My mother, still uneasy, prayed for Mijok's safe return, calling on the names of our ancestors and also on 'Nhialic', the name of God, a deity like the Christian God but named after the ancestors. We fused Christianity with our Dinka religion by believing that the ancestors and God were working together. Our prayers could only be answered if God and the ancestors were mentioned in conjunction. Finally rumours started to circulate that the group Mijok was fighting with were coming home. Sure enough, the following day they started marching into our village. Again everyone was excited. This time Mijok would return as the hero he had wanted to be. Some of the other soldiers were from our village, while others were from surrounding areas. I was excited at the thought that there was to be a huge celebration to welcome them all back.

As the soldiers marched in, wearing their green uniforms and carrying their AK47s, people were yelling out to those they knew. There were lots of hugs and tears as different families were reunited. My parents stood anxiously watching, then started asking where Mijok was. My father kept insisting that his son must be up the back of the long line straggling in. My mother wasn't so sure; immediately she felt sick to her stomach with the suspicion that something was wrong.

By the time the last soldier had marched in, Mijok was still nowhere to be seen. Now both of my parents were worried and my father was agitatedly asking where his son was. A few soldiers tried to calm him down, explaining that Mijok had been sent to another village and would return soon. That night all was quiet and I wondered what had happened to the celebration I had been expecting. The next morning we were doing all our usual chores. I was cleaning up after the cattle, and the little ones, Thonager and Athien, were nearby playing. Suddenly I heard a scream such as I had never heard before. It was my mother. A representative from the army had decided it was time to tell the truth. Mijok was dead.

We were told that he had gone to Bam, the town the SPLA was fighting for, only to find that the combat was all but done. Mijok and Duor Niang had been walking past a rundown house when they heard what sounded like a donkey and some goats inside. My uncle was about to look inside but Mijok insisted on going in first. He had drawn his gun and taken his first step through the door when he was shot and killed. Somehow my uncle managed to escape. Three others passing the same house weren't so lucky – they were shot soon after with bullets from Mijok's gun.

My mother raced out of the hut and started thrashing about. She was hitting anything and anyone that stood in her way; eventually she threw herself on the ground, pounding her hands into the dirt. She screamed: 'I want to die, I want to die!' The women of the village surrounded her; they were all in shock. Mijok was the first person from our circle to be killed in the war. Instead of trying to calm my mother down, the other women also started screaming. It was a noise I will never forget.

Over the next month the women cut their hair short and wore black as a sign of respect. The atmosphere in the village was different from anything I had ever known. The elders grew suspicious of each other, forming whispering factions. A lot of us did not believe he was dead. I thought it was some kind of joke – we were being tricked, and Mijok would one day turn up. Others were crying silently. My mother and her sisters shaved their heads and took off all their jewellery.

They tied a mourning rope around their wrists and wore dark clothes. The village was quiet: at that time there was no singing at night.

Although our village had been razed to the ground, Mijok was the first armed soldier from our sub-tribe to have been killed in the conflict. There was no funeral because we were never able to recover Mijok's body. The army said they had buried him somewhere, but were vague on the details. We had no ceremony of any kind. If we had the body of Mijok, he would have been wrapped and tied in animal skins, then buried about ten metres from the house in a three-metre-deep hole. We would have killed a cow or a goat, then cooked the meat on the spot, with everybody eating. As we didn't do any of these things, I felt both an emptiness and a continuing disbelief that he had really died.

It was another month before Monyleck came home and discovered what had happened to Mijok. Monyleck barely had time for it to sink in before he was sent off again to help collect children from the surrounding area to train in Ethiopia, just as he and Mijok had done. If Monyleck was distressed about Mijok he didn't show it – between being taught by our father to hide our emotions and his military training, he would have had a hard time expressing any strong emotion, let alone his reaction to the death of his closest brother.

By now Monyleck was devoted to his job and did as the army requested. He began recruiting children from around the area. He wouldn't go house to house, but would speak to elders and family leaders, instructing them to pick a son to supply to the army. Monyleck's role was to form them into groups and keep them together. Some families considered refusing, but if they did, Monyleck would harass them, and the SPLA would come and take their cows as punishment. He didn't try to 'sell' the idea with positive arguments such as how the SPLA would feed and educate us. The threat of losing cattle or being punished was usually enough. Some children from our village were taken, but most came from parts further out. In total just under 1000 children from our area of 96,000 people would be taken away from their families, possibly forever, to train as soldiers for the SPLA. Our family was lucky, as none of us was chosen – this time.

About a year later, in 1987, the SPLA again went from village to village, this time taking one child from each family. The families weren't given a choice – you had to give up a child or cattle were taken, arrests made and the child taken by force anyway. We knew that this time our family wouldn't be so lucky. Little did we know, however, that it would be Monyleck who would be given the responsibility of taking one of us. I was about ten at the time and a prime target.

My father was aware that Monyleck wanted me to go, but there were many heated discussions before a final choice was made. No one was happy. Monyleck was forced into a position of having to choose one of us. If he left our family alone the army would consider him to be favouring us. They didn't care that it was his own flesh and blood he was sending off to war. All they cared about was that he made up his quota and that the choice was evenly distributed throughout the villages. If he backed away from his responsibilities he would be killed and I would be taken anyway. I remember one night hearing my father and Monyleck arguing. We boys were sitting around one fire while the men were at another. I couldn't hear what they were saying but I knew it was about me, and I knew my father tried to protect me from the choice Monyleck had to make.

I could tell that my mother was fearful of me leaving. She was still grieving for Mijok. His loss had taken the shine from her eyes. The only comment I heard her make to Monyleck about me going was late one night when, in a bitter voice, she said: 'Why don't you just eat him?'

I had always thought my mother was naive when it came to the war and what happened when children were taken away. Whenever she saw an aeroplane flying overhead she would say it was full of children being taken to America as slaves. Maybe to her that was better than thinking about what really happened.

Monyleck tried to dodge the brutal truth by insisting that this was my chance to get an education and be looked after by the army. My mother may have been naive in some ways, but she didn't buy Monyleck's argument. To make matters worse, he also wanted my younger brother Thonager to go. At first I was in favour of this. I thought that if Thonager came with me it would be easier for me to face whatever was ahead. But it didn't take long before I realised he needed to stay with the family – it was bad enough that I would go, let alone a seven year old as well.

However, during the days that followed, I felt as though all my family's attention had shifted to protecting Thonager. I began to wonder if they cared that I was the one whose life was about to change forever.

In the end it was decided that Thonager was too young, too impatient and too prone to crying. He would cry when he was hungry, he would cry when he was tired. It would also be safe to say that he was the laziest of us all. He would often be found sleeping or drifting off to sleep while he was meant to be doing his chores – not a good quality in a soldier.

And so, the decision was made. I would go to Ethiopia – without Thonager.

In the days leading up to me leaving, I remember there being a lot of crying as different women from the village came to visit my mother. A lot of them understood what she was going through – they had sons who would be leaving too. I remember my father's frustration growing, and his temper shortened. He stopped talking to Monyleck altogether. I know that he was angry about what was happening to me, but I also wished that he could have softened and been kind to me in my last days.

Monyleck was busy preparing clothes for me to take: five pairs of shorts that he cut and stitched from a blue bedsheet. He told me how valuable they would be. I would be able to wear two pairs, while I could sell the other three along the way in order to buy food or, maybe even more importantly, friends to protect me.

Before I knew it Monyleck was leaving the village to prepare the rest of the group. He was to go to a temporary camp about two and a half hours' walk away in a place called Biu. Before he left, he gave me the shorts he had made along with advice on how to stay safe on my journey.

'Always do as you are told, keep your eyes open and remember that all decisions are now in your hands,' he said. 'You are responsible for yourself.'

Then, with as much care as he had given me his advice, he looked me straight in the eyes and told me: 'If you choose to run, if you escape from the army along the way, I will make it my duty to shoot and kill you.'

I knew he meant what he said. Our eyes were locked together. It was the first time that I – and Monyleck too, I think – recognised the full gravity of the situation. Monyleck needed me to understand that this wasn't a game. The furthest my imagination would stretch was to think this would be a quick adventure and I would be a big hero instantly. Monyleck could see this. He had to snap me into awareness of what was to come. He had even more at stake than I did. He would protect me as much as he could, but if I was seen to be favoured by him, or if I tried to run away, it would put him in danger from other members of the rebel army who would see him as weak. He was not the sort of brother who would put his own life at risk to save mine. That was what he was telling me. If it came to choosing between his own life and mine, he would save his own. After sitting in silence for a few minutes, he got up and left.

About two days before I was to leave, my family decided to pay a visit to the spiritual leader of our community. Beny Wian lived about ten minutes from us and had the largest hut in the village. His was the place that the people of our village would go to in order to connect at the highest level to our ancestors. He had inherited this position when Makuei Bilkuei, my great-uncle, had died in 1978. Beny Wian was one of Makuei's nephews. As at the tree outside our home, sacrifices would be made here to please the ancestors. Many of us children were afraid of him. To me he looked frightening; it felt as though he had a power about him which, although he used it for good, was unnatural.

Beny Wian always wore a red sheet wrapped around his shoulders. His hair was a big afro streaked with grey. As usual he sat silently, knowing that everyone in the village was a bit scared of him, and carried a long spear, straight as a toothpick. My family and other members of our village prayed for my protection and safe return home. It still didn't seem real to me: I couldn't help feeling that the prayers were for someone else. It hadn't sunk in that I was the one in danger. As the sacrifice was made I felt strangely safe, somehow more grown up and impor- tant, because so many people were looking out for me.

With Monyleck gone, time was speeding along. I can barely remember what happened in the last few days, but the night before I left is very clear in my memory. Perhaps that's because it would be the last night of my childhood. I remember sitting alone in the yard where we kept our cattle, where I had spent so many days working and playing, thinking about was going to happen and how I would handle myself. I kept thinking of Monyleck's threat. I could hardly think of anything else. My heart was racing and, to make matters worse, while I tried to say goodbye to my friends they were all talking about the things they would do the next day. I wanted to say, 'But tomorrow I won't be here any more!'

Preparations had begun for my farewell. People came from all around – about forty of them, from the extended Bilkuei family. They brought food, drums and a never-ending trail of advice about how I should undertake my journey. As the drums started beating, a friend of mine, Thon Bil, began to sing. He was the best singer in the village. Usually he would lead the singing, with everyone else repeating phrases in chorus around him. I was always envious of his voice. I wanted to be musical, to have some kind of talent, but I was too shy. Thon's voice gave him a degree of leadership beyond his age and a respect that was otherwise hard to earn.

As his voice sang out over the village and the intensity of the drums built, the mood of the night became charged with grief. Women were crying, my mother was crying, and of course Thonager was crying! My father just looked angry, not with me but with the world.

My father was a superstitious man, so at the climax of all the emotional outpouring he chose to perform a ceremony to see what the ancestors really had to say about me leaving. To perform this ceremony he needed a special stick, one metre long, with a metal spearhead at one end and a ball-shaped knob at the other. It was carved smooth along the sides and had a string of beads tied at the neck of the knob. My father would throw the stick in the air, wait for it to land and see what direction the sharp end fell. If it fell with the sharp end facing him, I would return home safely. If the sharp end pointed away from him, it would mean that I would not return and therefore did not have the protection of my ancestors, despite all our prayers.

Everyone fell silent as my father quietly prayed before throwing the stick. With a steady hand he threw it into the air. Everyone's eyes followed it as it flew up, twisted around, then fell to the ground – the blunt end towards my father.

It was not a good sign. Not one to give up, my father picked up the stick, told Thonager to fetch some water from the stream and continued to pray. This time his face was intense, his eyes wide open and staring at me. When my younger brother returned, my father blessed the stick by sprinkling it with the fresh water. He then splashed water over me in order to cleanse me and make me more acceptable to the ancestors. When he was done he was ready to throw the stick again.

For a second time the voices and drums fell silent and we all watched as the stick rose, then fell – blunt end towards my father. He was not a happy man. Still not willing to give up, he ordered Thonager to fetch one of our goats. He decided that the ancestors needed to know of his devotion to them, and if they couldn't see it yet, they would by the time he made yet another sacrifice in their honour.

Thonager returned with the goat. It was as if the goat knew what was about to happen, and in its eyes I could see my own fear. The drumming started up again, layered with voices that could have come from heaven singing a traditional song of praise. I had witnessed many sacrifices throughout my child-hood, but for the first time I felt for the animal about to die. The goat's eyes were wide with terror as the knife, sharpened and ready, was placed against its stretched throat.

My father was begging the ancestors: 'I kill this goat for you, to make you happy. Protect my son!'

I closed my eyes as the sacrifice was made. The goat's blood was used to make a cross on my forehead. It was not a Christian cross; our religious education was purely traditional, bound up with our ancestors. The only ones in the family with any Christian education were my father and Monyleck, who had been taken to churches in Bentiu. Monyleck, christened Matthew, believed in Christian religion – after he had been to school, he thought our traditional beliefs carried something evil.

My father slit the goat across its stomach, then reached inside its still-warm body and removed undigested grass which he then sprayed over me. He did this so that the blessing, if given, would have a physical presence on my body. It would become a part of me, travelling where I travelled, and it would remind the ancestors of their promise to protect me.

The same water that had been sprinkled over me before was used to wash the stick. My father was now ready for his third attempt. A third failure would prove to him that there was no protection from the ancestors and I would be unlikely to return my father alive.

I could feel his desperation as he held the stick ready to throw. He held it by the neck of the sharp end, between his thumb and forefinger. His beliefs were my beliefs, so I, too, was anxious to see my fate revealed. With everyone's eyes focused on it, the stick flew through the air, higher than before, taking longer to land.

As it fell, I was so tense I closed my eyes. No sooner had my eyes closed than I could hear what sounded like an eruption, voices screaming, cheering – the sharp end was pointing towards my father! I would go with the blessing of my ancestors.

The rest of the night was a strange combination of celebration over the blessing mixed with the realisation that the next day I would be leaving my childhood behind me for a life in the army. Almost everyone had advice. One by one, throughout the night, they came to share their wisdom with me. By the end of the night I felt so overwhelmed I didn't know what I was thinking or feeling. All I knew was that my time had come so quickly that I had forgotten to ask my parents for more time to play. I knew that by daylight I would be a man, and I would no longer have room in my life for playing, for being a child.

The night grew still as friends and family started to leave. In the end it was just my parents and me. Thonager had tried to stay awake in an effort to spend as much time as possible with me, but his sagging eyes were ready for dreaming. In the quiet that followed, my father told me of how he had gone away to fight when he was young and how he was living proof of the protection and guidance that our ancestors provided. He had fought for seventeen years before returning home. I wondered if my journey would last that long.

I looked towards my mother. Even after all that had happened, I only wanted one thing: I wanted her to say I didn't have to go. I could tell she wanted me to stay, but her silence told me that she was as powerless as I was. She just sat with a glazed look in her eyes.

I tried to sleep that night but all I could do was lie awake thinking about what would happen to me. My father might have survived the army, but what about Mijok? Where were the ancestors when it came time to protect him? As I thought of Mijok I wanted to run and hide, but the threat of Monyleck putting a gun to my head froze me to the ground.

By the time morning came around, I had talked myself into excitement. I had to think of it as an adventure. Today I would celebrate becoming a man.

As I prepared to leave, the rest of the village again joined my family. There was a lot of crying. Six of my cousins, as well as countless others from the village, would form the group that would escort me to the temporary camp where Monyleck was waiting. My supplies consisted of a jerry can filled with water, a blanket I carried in a nylon sack the army gave me, and the shorts that Monyleck had made. I was wearing nothing but the shorts and some cowskin slippers my mother had cut and sewn to fit my feet. A soldier arrived to take us to the first camp. He was given a thousand Sudanese pounds – a large amount, enough to buy four head of cattle – to look after me and my cousins: Bol, Wour, Angok, Chol, Ngor and Mayer. The blanket was meant to cover all seven of us.

I said goodbye to my grandmother, who as usual had my beautiful baby sister Athien by her side.

Everyone in the village thought my grandmother possessed magical healing powers and had a strong connection to our ancestors – strong enough that she could hear their voices telling her what would happen in the future.

My grandmother said to me, 'Go, you will be all right.'

As she held my hand I felt calmer. Her powers helped to take away some of my fears. If she said I would be all right, I felt I would be. Athien smiled at me as if to confirm the deal. I smiled back and went to join the group to leave.

The sun was going down and everyone was already moving. There was an early winter chill falling with the dusk. It took me a minute before I realised we were walking out of the village. The other boys who had been selected were with us now. People were standing by the side of the track, singing and yelling out messages of support, telling us how strong we were, how brave we were, their voices lifting me out of my childhood and into my adulthood.

Thonager was running alongside, crying out, 'I want to go with you, let me go!'

I kept yelling in return, 'I'll be back, I'll be back!'

My mother was going to walk all the way to the camp with me, so I would not have to say goodbye to her yet. Monyleck was going to escort us for the first week of our march, and he had told my mother that she could come as far as he was going, and then he would bring her back.

As we got further along the track, the voices from the village thinned out. I didn't feel as though I had said goodbye to anyone properly along the way. I was losing friends and family in the crowd, I was struggling to keep up, it had all happened too fast.

The time came to say goodbye to my father, when he and Thonager stopped on the track. I remembered the conversation I had had with him when I was younger, when he told me that no man was born at the same time as his father, so therefore no man should rely on his father always being there. I felt proud that I was strong enough to leave and become my own man, even though it wasn't by choice.

I don't remember us saying anything to each other. With one last wave, I walked around a corner and they were gone.

As we left the village environs, my confidence wavered. It was growing dark fast. Walking along beside me, my mother started to talk to me, telling me that I was her favourite son.

'When I grow old you'll look after me,' she said.

I smiled and thought about the countless times when I'd been hungry and she had joked that I was not her son at all, so she didn't have to feed me. Then she'd give in. It had been her favourite joke with me and always made me laugh. As we walked my mind started to drift. I thought about all the things I could have been doing – hunting, fishing, swimming. I pushed these thoughts to the back of my mind and tried to concentrate on seeing Monyleck. For all the harsh things that had been said between us, he was still my brother. He would be my anchor, at least for the first stage. Monyleck's role was in recruiting us, not training us, so he would help guide us towards Ethiopia before turning around and coming to serve closer to home.

As we drew close to Biu I could see other groups of children who had been drawn from different areas marching into the village. I had relatives who lived there, so it wasn't too strange to me: it had been the home of my great-uncle, Makuei Bilkuei. As we entered, we passed some village huts on the outskirts and the ruins of an old schoolhouse that had been built by the British. Now it had been stripped of its red bricks and all that was standing was the frame.

We passed a line of wells, and then came to the centre of Biu – a wooded plateau where the Makuei family lived. I could see the lights of cooking fires dotted around the huts. I heard Monyleck barking orders, telling people where to stand. As our group was shuffled into position at the rear of the camp he started to call our names, then directed us where to go next.

I was the last person he looked at. There was no smile, no warmth. He was like a different person, as if he didn't want anyone to know that we were related, even though our mother was standing right by me.

He called my name with the same cold efficiency as he'd called everyone else's. I looked up at my mother's face. She gestured for me to go; she didn't hug me. I didn't want her to hug me. I thought if she had, I would have cried, and right now I needed to be a man. I needed all the other kids in the camp to respect me. I moved towards Monyleck who pointed me sharply in the direction of a group of about thirty children, who would be my basic unit, or *basila*. As I looked around, I was struck by how many others there were: about five hundred all up. I held my head high and tried my best to look confident but I couldn't help noticing how different Monyleck was, with his gun slung over his shoulder, shouting orders. I realised that having my brother with me wouldn't make my journey any easier. If anything, I thought, it might make it harder.

The evening parade was already finished, and we weren't going to form up again until the morning. So the group dispersed to sleep the night. I went with my mother to the hut of one of my Malkuei uncles, where we slept.

In the morning I rejoined my *basila* and we were introduced to each other and formed into ranks for the first parade of the day. All of a sudden the *panan*, the music leader, started a chorus: 'We are now with you.'

Everyone sang back: 'We are now with you.'

It wasn't like the singing in the village. This was much more for show, mainly to display our loyalty. There would be a lot of singing to come – it was designed to create a sense of normality and it would be one way in which our group would bond.

Our first song together was short and followed immediately by a speech.

Monyleck started: 'Here there are no children. Put your childish ways behind you. You are men, you are army men. You are soldiers.'

I could tell that some of the kids were scared, as they didn't have their mothers with them. I was lucky. My mother was standing right behind me.

After the speech we began to move out – our journey to Ethiopia was underway. We had been told it would take two or three months. Instantly it hit me: how would we walk all that way? What would we do for food? How safe were we going to be? My mind flooded with questions and doubts.

We left Biu as the morning mist was lifting. We followed a winding dirt path through open, flat grasslands. Although the terrain was easy, the walk was slow, as each village we passed through wanted to contribute some gift to the group. Our village had given a cow which Monyleck had bought to camp with him, and now we had fifteen cows all up. Some villages donated maize, beans and other vegetables to cook along the way. At least that answered one of my questions.

At first we marched in our *basila* but after a few hours we had broken into fragments: the strongest walkers at the front, the tired ones drifting to the back. My mother walked at the side of the track and tried her best to keep up with me. As the day dragged on I started thinking about stories I had heard of people being killed in the war, not just Mijok but others. I had never been more than two days' walk from my village, when we'd escaped to the Nile. Now we were venturing further and further into the unknown. I became paranoid as the sounds of the bush grew more and more unfamiliar. Bats cried out during the day and night, and there were animal sounds I'd never heard before. We saw a lot of vultures circling in the sky, a sure sign that there were lions and other predators about. I tried my best to hold faith with the blessings that my ancestors had given me, and told myself that I would return home soon enough.

The day grew hotter and the track more narrow. We ended up walking in single file, taking a break every couple of hours. We tried not to make too much noise. Every time we were to rest, the signal would be given by a tap on the shoulder. As each new person was tapped they sat down – we were like dominoes. Each rest was short. With another tap on the shoulder we were up and moving again.

By late afternoon we came to a stream, about a hundred metres wide, which would be our camp for the night. We were split into two groups: one would cross the river now and the other would follow the next morning. The river had a strong current and was infested with crocodiles. We saw snakes around the edges of the water. Before entering the river Monyleck aimed his gun towards where we would cross and shot into the water numerous times. Satisfied that he had scared off the crocodiles, he ushered the first group across. This was my group.

My mother was not allowed to cross the river that afternoon. She would spend the night on this side and follow me across the next morning.

There was a raft waiting by the bank, made from branches bound together by rope, but it was too small to take us all. One of the leaders said, 'If you can swim, swim.' Some of the older boys swam bravely across, a few of them almost carrying friends with them. I couldn't swim across a river like that, and I was afraid of the crocodiles, so I waited for my turn on the raft. Of my cousins, Wour was the only one big and strong and brave enough to swim. The others came on the raft with me.

After I got to the far bank, groups on both sides were given jobs to do before nightfall. Soldiers patrolled the fringes, to make sure nobody ran away. I had to collect firewood, while others made a clearing for a night-time shelter. As the evening meal was cooked, I sat looking towards the other side of the river and wondered if being separated from my mother would always feel this bad.

The next morning, when everyone had crossed the river, my mother included, the journey continued. We walked for two more days, stopping at different villages. Each village would be asked to contribute by supplying us with food and extra supplies. Some were happy to help, but others were unimpressed at having to share what little food they had. None, however, refused us. They were intimidated. They knew it would be taken by force anyway. We were moving into Shilluk land – a different people from the Dinka. They marked their foreheads with small incisions rather than long straight scars. The adults wore sheets knotted at their shoulders and hanging down low to their knees. They didn't keep as many cattle as we did, and being riverside people they lived by their fishing. As they spoke Shilluk rather than Dinka, we had to communicate by sign language. It was a new world for me, and mostly I was scared. There were many armed bands about, and we were not a strong group. Other army groups were known to attack each other, and I was afraid that these people who spoke different languages could be our enemies. They might have hidden guns. We could be attacked at any time. I was constantly insecure.

My mother and Monyleck were about to end their part of the journey. I was grateful that they had at least come this far, but was scared about the prospect of being on my own.

The night before she left, my mother cooked some meat in soup for my six cousins, Monyleck and me. Her meals were always better than the bean stews the army cooked, of course, but this one was the best meal I'd ever eaten. She told us we would all be safe and reminded me of the protection the ancestors had granted me. Monyleck added to her words of comfort, but just as he'd done with me back in the village, he told us all that if we decided to run away after he left, he would track us down and shoot us. With that thought we tried to go to sleep. I stayed awake for a very long time, wondering what it would be like to continue on to Ethiopia alone.

Early the next morning, Monyleck and my mother turned back towards home, and our group started moving onwards. It was a strange parting. There were no tearful farewells. My mother simply said, 'Go well.' Then she called me 'Chol-*dit*', which made me feel special. Attaching '*dit*' to my name meant a respect usually reserved for grown-ups. I could feel my shoulders straighten and I raised my head high. To have the respect of my mother was all I needed to continue my journey as a true adult, capable of looking after myself.

My mother didn't hug me or kiss me goodbye; she just walked off into the distance. I didn't want to hug or kiss her, as I felt I had to control myself to appear manly. To give way to my emotions might have let loose an unstoppable flood. If I had cried, she would have cried, and that would set me crying even more. The other boys would then start teasing me or otherwise make my life hard. So I distanced myself and watched her walk away. I felt strongly that it would be the last time I would see her, and it was. Later that night, when I was lying down and meant to be sleeping, I let some of my thoughts come through. But I grew so sad, I forced myself not to think about her. I tried to pretend that nothing significant was happening. I would practise this repression of my feelings for many years, and it was nearly a decade later, when I was in South Africa and began watching a lot of TV and seeing kids with families, that I began to understand truly how I was missing my own family. For most of my journey I would be similar to the others around me, who had also lost their mothers, so I wouldn't feel too sorry for myself. But in South Africa, when I saw boys my age with families, what had happened to me so many years before would hit me with full force.

CHAPTER 2

Ethiopia

FOR THE REST OF OUR JOURNEY TO ETHIOPIA, my closest companion would be my older cousin, Thomas Wour Kuol, the biggest of the six and the strongest. Often we smaller boys were picked on to do the hardest jobs, such as carrying the cooking pots or a big bag of maize, or the endless routine of collecting water and firewood, but Wour would step in and shoulder the load for us, even though he didn't have to. He was about fourteen, a few years older than me. He hated the name Thomas and insisted that everyone call him Wour. When we were growing up he was one of my few cousins who would let me go with him when he hunted. The others all pushed me away, but he never did. Just as he had done then, he would look out for me now.

Our march took us through unvarying flat land, with loamy soil that was not being cultivated because it was the dry season. This country was not much different from where I had grown up. Everybody was tired. On a typical day, we walked in the late afternoon and early evening, stopped at around 11pm, cooked and slept a while, then started again at dawn, resting in the middle of the day for a couple of hours. A lot of the boys didn't have shoes, and would fall behind. While those of us at the front rested, the slower ones caught up. A lot of them got sick, and all I could do to help was to share their load and rest with them. They suffered from weakness, stomach problems, coughing, mosquito-borne illnesses, and diarrhoea. Our group became very slow and sometimes weaker boys got too sick to go on. They would be left behind in villages, either alone or with a friend.

We continued to stop at villages along the way to Ethiopia, asking for food and shelter where we could. Our main source of food was the cattle we brought with us. Every few days we slaughtered and butchered a cow. At one village, where we stopped overnight, there was an uneasy feeling: we weren't sure of how welcome we really were. In the morning we woke to find that our cattle had all been stolen. Everyone panicked. We had planned to use the remaining cows for milk, to eat, or to sell along the way to buy other things such as goats or grain.

No one in the village was telling us what had happened overnight. We'd all been so tired from walking that no one had stayed awake to protect the cattle from theft. Now someone would have to pay. The boys whose job it was to stay awake were humiliated and beaten, while the leaders interrogated the villagers. The argument went on but the villagers were silent and eventually we had to continue our journey without our food supply. Before long we were close to starvation. What villages we did come across were now obliged to feed us.

When the cattle were stolen, Mayer said we should run back the way we'd come. He talked about how we could fish and dance and play, how good life was back home in our village. Bol and some of the younger boys began crying. We were already weak and upset from losing the cattle, and now Mayer was pulling on our heartstrings. 'If we go fast for four days,' he said, 'we can catch up with Monyleck and go home with him.'

Wour wasn't enthusiastic about this. Being the oldest and biggest, he would receive the brunt of the punishment if we were caught deserting. He looked at me suspiciously, seeing which way I would go.

I reminded my cousins of what Monyleck had said: if he caught us deserting, he would kill us or return us to the army. We had no choice, I said; better to take the pain all at once than to try to escape and have to go through it all again. Also, I said, our families would not be very happy to see us if we'd deserted. We might be bringing them all kinds of trouble.

Wour was pleased to see I'd taken his side. Mayer was just as big as Wour, but had a weaker heart. I was showing Wour that I was as brave as he was.

As time went on the days all seemed the same. Wake, walk, rest, continue, eat, sleep. My cowskin slippers lasted two months. I kept trying to tie them together, but eventually copied the idea some boys had had of tying old T-shirts around their feet. The ground was sharp with hard mud, cut up by cattle hoofprints and then dried, very rough. There were not many rocks, but sticks and roots poked through, and thorns. My feet cracked in parallel lines across my soles. They blistered and bled. There was no water to wash the cuts, so they got infected. Soon I would be limping along on my heels or toes, trying to find a part of my foot that wasn't hurting. Like most of the boys, I walked with a long staff to support myself, bent like an old man.

We were afraid of being attacked by government soldiers or militia, so we began to sit in the shade and doze for most of the day, and then do our walking at night. We had no light but what was cast by the moon and the stars. The tactic worked, at least. No one attacked us along the way.

Food was our incentive. Normally our meal consisted of some maize mixed with beans in a gruel. We scooped it out of bullet boxes, which were our bowls. We ate twice a day, a little bit early in the morning and then more in the evening. If we arrived very late, sometimes we were too tired to eat. If you could stay awake, you'd cook. As long as we were getting something, we didn't think of the better food we'd had back home or what we were missing out on. But sometimes we went twenty-four hours without food, and it was every boy for himself, selling clothes or anything of value that you had for some scrap of food. When we had nothing, some boys would start talking about what people at home would be eating or drinking at this time of day. They did this to see if they could make other boys cry. It was a kind of bullying and also a way of spreading discontent, because the boys who were doing the taunting wanted to run away but feared doing it alone. Their objective in causing unrest was to goad the others into running away in a group. It never worked. Our leaders kept telling us that if we went a little bit further, there would be good food waiting for us. They always lied to us about how far we had to go, they always let us down, but we had no choice but to keep going.

One day we stopped at a local elder's hut in the area of Dong Jol. Locally this man was considered an *ayong dit*, a magician with psychic powers. We heard he had predicted that two bombs would fall in the area, but no one would be hurt and the bombs would be wasted. The leaders of our group asked him to perform a ceremony to help us on our way. He ordered swathes of grass to be parted to form a path and a rope-like material stretched at waist height for us to jump over. We would all have to jump the rope without touching it in order to receive his blessing to continue our journey safely. All but one of us jumped successfully. A boy called Miakol Deng failed.

The next day, we heard planes flying in the distance. We were told they were Antonov bombers sent by the government. We never actually saw them, because they were so high. Just as the magician had predicted, they dropped two bombs. Neither

46

hit the village and as far as I know no one died. The following week Miakol Deng went missing and we never saw him again.

At the time Miakol disappeared, we were closer to Ethiopia than to our villages. We were all getting very tired. As we were sometimes tempted by villagers' offers to take us in, most of us thought Miakol might have run off to be employed or exploited by a local villager to do their work for them. Others thought he had been killed by villagers, and robbed, or taken by wildlife. If he'd run into the forest, a lion or hyena might have attacked him. Later in life, I met a lot of people who had known Miakol, but I never heard anyone say they had any knowledge of what had happened to him. He had disappeared into thin air.

It was in a village called Wutlang that an old woman made an offer to my cousin Chol and me. When we entered strange villages, we usually spread out to the huts to ask for food. This old woman looked after us very well, giving us lots to eat. After one meal, she said: 'Come and stay with me, you two can be my sons. You can look after my cattle and I will find wives for you.'

We made agreeable sounds, because she was feeding us so well. But when it came time to form up again in our *basila*, there was no question of staying. Why would we walk all this way just to stay in a village like Wutlang, where we didn't know anybody, to look after an old lady? As nice as she had been, we had no intention of becoming her sons. As we gathered to march out, I noticed Chol was burying his face in his T-shirt. I looked to the side of the path and saw the old woman, searching for her 'sons'. I left Wutlang with my face hidden behind my hand.

Later, Chol and I talked about the woman. I found her very strange, and not credible. Chol was tempted to believe her. As I ran the scenario around and around in my mind, I was thinking: 'I already have all these things, cattle and land, back at home, so why would I want to set up a life here?' It scared me – like she was asking me to abandon my own family. But as we were so afraid of something going wrong, and as we wanted the food she was offering, we had played along to keep the peace and now we were out of the village, we were relieved most of all that we had escaped without causing any big problems.

Another month would roll on before we reached Nasir, a small town on the Sudanese side of the Ethiopian border. Before we arrived, we were warned that the government army had tried to seize the town, but failed. We were about to see just how devastating war could be.

The SPLA were now patrolling Nasir's borders. What little remained of the town was a mess. All the buildings, whether they were made of brick, mud or thatch, had been burnt down. A few were left in ruins. As we entered Nasir the overwhelming smell of death hit us. There were trenches everywhere, many lined with dead bodies rotting in the heat of the sun. As we marched through the town many of us were physically sick, not only from the stench but from the terror of not knowing what we were walking into. The town was eerily quiet at first, but every now and then we would come across someone weeping over a dead soldier or civilian. As I looked at the bodies I wondered if I, too, would end up in a trench with my friends. I tried not to look at the faces of the dead but I couldn't help noticing one boy who seemed to be around my age. His face was calm. To an extent it gave me comfort: at least in death he had managed to find peace. As I moved on I chose to look up at the cloudless blue sky, the only thing that seemed clean and untouched.

We didn't know it then, but along with the trenches that had been dug through the town there were also underground dugouts in which Arab soldiers from the government army were still hiding, waiting for the SPLA to move out. We never saw them. The fighting seemed to be over and for the duration of our stay we didn't see any further bloodshed. It wasn't until we had long gone that we heard that the fighting had resumed when these Arab soldiers emerged. I wondered how the surviving people of the town could cope with even one more loss. I didn't want to think about how many more people were killed after we left.

It took us a day to walk through Nasir, the trip made slower by the care needed to avoid the landmines that riddled the town. The government had planted mines inside Nasir, while the SPLA had planted mines outside. They were each trying to trap the other.

We went through in single file, with an SPLA officer in front who had already been in the town and established a safe path for us to follow. He gave us strict orders to stay in line, and we snaked through the town. Half a metre either side could mean death.

By nightfall, safely on the other side of Nasir, I felt exhausted. With the image of so many dead burnt into my memory and the smell still lingering, I thought of my family back home. I thought mainly of how my father had been so tough on us and why it now made sense. I couldn't imagine having seen the images I saw that day without the preparation I'd been given. As we readied to sleep, I could see others who were still shaking. We had all seen the carnage, but no one wanted to talk about it. In Dinka culture, it was considered bad luck for young people to talk about death. Looking back on it, I think we were also traumatised by what we had seen. The SPLA showed us no concern. There was certainly no counselling! Among ourselves, we might go so far as to say, 'Did you see that body?', but for a lot of us, it was the first time we had seen dead people. The SPLA had told us from the beginning that we were on our own – no mum or dad; we were army and we'd be treated as army. An experience like Nasir was treated as part of our induction, as if we were going to have to get used to this. I felt very alone. As I lay down to sleep that night, I wondered how the others in my *basila* had grown up and what their fathers had done to prepare them. I thought about the ceremony I had undergone, with my father and the stick, and how I had passed the test. I felt safe enough to sleep for the night.

We had left Baal, the place of my birth, in December 1987, and had now been walking for more than three months. My feet were sore and covered in cuts and blisters. My shoes had fallen apart and I was walking barefoot. A lot of the time we walked through mud, and some boys got bad infections in their feet like had. We had lived on stews of maize, beans and water, shared among too many to satisfy any of us. By now, a lot of boys were ill. But in the army, if you could still eat, you were not treated as sick. The SPLA didn't consider malaria or diorrhoea to be a sickness. An infection in your foot, as long as you could walk, was not treated as serious. The only sickness they would recognise was one that stopped you eating. Some boys got into that state, not eating for a day or so, but they would recover and keep stumbling along.

A day after Nasir we arrived at the military barracks in Jokmiir, a logistical centre for the SPLA. I met two of my uncles here, Dau Ngor and Deng Mayer. They were on their way back from Ethiopia where they had been training. Dau Ngor was my father's brother, while Deng Mayer was my father's cousin. We only had a few minutes to talk to them, most of which we spent exchanging greetings, but when we said we were going to Ethiopia they grimaced and said, 'You boys are too young to go there.' But they could see it was inevitable, and didn't want to make us feel too scared, so they said in farewell, 'It's close, not too far now.'

The barracks in Jokmiir were extensive, and no civilians seemed to live there: it was all SPLA.

Jokmiir had no big buildings, just a scattering of mud houses and big khaki tents where they stored ammunition. I'd never seen a real army camp before, and was curious to see how the SPLA was set up. But this was only an arms dump, with no more than a hundred soldiers staying there.

Here our journey would take a new twist. We were cooking in the barracks area when there was a great machine noise and someone shouted, 'Come outside!'

We all stood, our eyes wide with excitement. It seemed we wouldn't have to walk across the border into Ethiopia – we would fly by helicopter! I had seen a helicopter flying in the air before but this was the first time I'd seen one up close. Never had I imagined I would fly in one. The helicopter was painted in khaki camouflage. Its enormous noise made me afraid, and I didn't dare go anywhere near the blades, which were blowing dust everywhere. The engine remained switched on, and men were running around shouting, as if they were all thrown into chaos by this terrifying machine.

As the base commander told us what was going to happen and who would fly first, some of the other boys surged towards the helicopter. They were beaten back by soldiers who quickly re-established order. The commander continued telling us that we were now on our way to Gambela in Ethiopia, the last stop before reaching our ultimate destination, Pinyudo. He praised us for getting as far as we had, then told us how our new life in Pinyudo would be worth our long journey. Seeing that our energy and morale were flagging, he said Pinyudo was a good place where a lot of other Sudanese boys like us were living and studying. 'Everything you need is there,' he said, 'food, clothing and housing. It will be better than where you have come from.' Pinyudo was our final destination, he said, and we would make friends there. (He didn't promise that we'd meet any of our relatives – the SPLA didn't want us to strengthen our family ties.)

When he finished his speech it was time for us to be split into groups to board the helicopter. Again some of the others let their excitement carry them away, rushing towards the loading zone. My cousin Wour, however, seemed to become afraid and ran towards the back of the group. The blades were in motion and this time I was swept up in the surge of those moving forward. I tripped and stumbled to the ground as others continued to run over the top of me. I was afraid that if they continued someone would end up being shot. The next thing I knew, I was being picked up and thrown into the helicopter. I could hear yelling over the sound of the blades as the soldiers finally got the others to settle.

More children were herded into the helicopter; we were like cargo, there were no seats, it was just an empty shell. As the rest of the group screamed to be let on board, the doors were slammed shut and before I knew it we were lifting off. The petrol smell was overpowering and we couldn't hear anything but the chopping of the blades and the scream of the engine. I scrambled to a window and looked out. I could feel my heart pound as the earth seemed to drop below us. I could see cows and huts, plains of grass and tracks that went forever. Others, too, were looking, while Bol was immediately sick, throwing up within minutes of taking off.

For most of the flight, I was too scared to look. I'd pop my head up against the window but didn't look down for more than a few seconds. Like many of the boys, as soon as I took a look I would recoil. It was so far down. The helicopter was also flying erratically, throwing my stomach all over the place.

I have no idea how long we were in the air, but as we descended I knew that we had arrived in Ethiopia.

***

Gambela was different from the flatness of home. Here we were in the mountains and the air smelt of spice. Everyone was in uniform. The soldiers scared me at first – their skin was lighter than mine and at first sight I thought they might have been Arabs. There was a lot of saluting and everything seemed very formal.

No sooner had we landed than the helicopter took off to pick up the next group. It would ferry back and forth throughout the day until most of our group was across the border. Wour, who avoided the helicopter ride, had to walk to reach us. With delays, it would take him two weeks.

Gambela wasn't a very relaxed atmosphere, with guards watching our every step. The military compound was surrounded by a tall metal fence, parts of which were topped with grass. I would soon learn that the smell of spice came from the food that was cooked on site. For the first time in a long time, we would eat something other than maize and beans.

The food was stored in what the SPLA called its 'consulate' in Gambela. We arrived hungry, but there was almost too much food. We were all warned not to eat too much, but some of us, including me, didn't listen. Our bellies bloated and the sudden change in diet made me sick. The maize was more finely ground than I'd been having, into a pap, and was served with beans or lentils seasoned with oil and salt. It was clean and well prepared, but our stomachs were not used to it.

While eating, I watched the Ethiopians who were there. They were shorter and more lightly built than us. They were much better equipped and wore cleaner uniforms, and their barracks were bigger and newer. They didn't speak our language, and shouted all the time instead of just talking.

We stayed in Gambela for two weeks waiting for our orders. During our last few days there, some of the others grew restless. By now everyone just wanted to move on and finish the journey. Many of us were excited to leave this camp for our ultimate destination, Pinyudo. Lots of kids were talking about what they imagined the camp would be like. So far we hadn't been told anything bad about Pinyudo; if anything, it sounded like a wonderful place. We knew that it was a military camp, and of course our families weren't there, but by now we were resigned to our status as soldiers and it felt almost as though we were heading to our new home. Having been broken down by the gruelling months of walking out of Sudan, we were willing to put the brightest gloss on anything that seemed even a little bit better.

There was one stop before Pinyudo: a market town called Itang. I was amazed by this place. It was the first time I'd seen anything like it. There was row after row of open-air market stalls. Most were covered in cheap sheets and grey or black blankets supported by wooden poles. The United Nations sign was displayed everywhere, as this was a UN-sponsored distribution centre. But really it was chaos. Everyone was shouting over the top of each other, advertising their products. Everywhere you looked there were people selling all kinds of things – tomatoes, sugar, fish, Sudanese beer (called *mou*), clothes, shoes. It seemed to me as though you could buy just about anything. I was over-whelmed, not only by the amount of people and the noise and the size, but by the smell. The whole place stank like a giant butcher shop full of rotting meat. The stink was carried on the thick smoke that rose from stoves and fires at what seemed like every second stall.

To make it worse, there were no toilets anywhere. Everyone had to use the bush that surrounded the markets as a huge human waste dump. The resulting stench was at its worst when the sky cleared after fresh rain showers. As the clouds parted and the sun hit, steam would lift the odour of faeces from the ground. Flies were everywhere. The rain also washed the effluent on the ground into the river, making the water dangerous to all those who swam in it, bathed in it and drank from it. Most people got their drinking water from taps that were connected to spear pipes into the ground. They would queue like sheep to get their share, but the water was also the source of terrible disease. It was being carried in from the river, scooped up from the same areas where everyone was washing and going to the toilet.

Despite the smell, Itang's markets had an atmosphere that I found irresistible. It was the biggest and busiest and most colourful place I had ever seen, and I was rejuvenated by it. It carried a sense of excitement and, to a degree, danger. There were always people running, yelling, screaming. The markets were patrolled by a lot of police, both Sudanese and Ethiopian. Outside the markets there was a prison: a small mud block with a thatched grass roof and a door that was fashioned out of small oil containers that had been flattened and cut and reconstructed as a sheet of metal.

The police's main problem was controlling the scores of children who had escaped from various army camps and were now alone and running amok. Some had found work bringing water from the river in thirty-litre jerry cans, selling it to survive, but most of them went around robbing and harassing people. Some had guns and would attack and rape girls. They used to sniff glue, smoke weed and drink alcohol.

These kids couldn't be controlled by anybody – they'd gone feral. They were very scary, because they had had some army training and were skilled in violence, skills they were using to survive. They worked the market and knew how to use money. They'd attack you if they thought you had something they wanted, especially if you were young. But my friends and I, seeing that they could afford good leather soccer balls, would push down our fears and play football games with them. I felt sorry for these children, as they were about my age and were heading for jail. If they were arrested for rape or for stealing, they would have their hands or legs cut off. I saw at least ten boys, sixteen or seventeen years old, walking around with scar tissue over their wrists where their hands had been. If they were stupid enough to commit another crime, there was no mercy: they would lose their other hand. I saw young men with no hands. Nobody pitied them. If both of their hands had been cut off, it was obvious they were thieves, and they would be treated like criminals for the rest of their lives. It would be better for them to move to somewhere where nobody knew them.

I remember one of these young men in particular. He was about eighteen years old, tall, light-skinned, with eyes that were always as red as fire. He was like a tiger, wild and unafraid of anything. The first time I saw him, he was pickpocketing an old woman. He saw me watching and came up and stood right beside me. He stared at me with his angry eyes and I knew that if I said a word I would be in trouble.

A little while later we heard that some of the boys who had been terrorising Itang had been arrested and sent to prison. The next time I saw that wild boy, weeks later, he had become quiet and timid. He looked scared of everything. He wasn't talking to anyone. Now that he wasn't a threat, I became almost friendly with him. I felt sorry for him but I knew to still keep my distance.

For us in the military, Itang had a purpose. It was a feeding centre designed to nurse us back to health after our months of walking. There was a hospital where we were weighed, and had our health checked and our ages estimated. Everyone loved being in that hospital. It was the first time since I had started the march that I felt truly looked after. Having said that, when I'd arrived in Itang the bones were showing through my skin, especially the ribs, so for me the stay may have seemed better than for those others who had not lost so much weight. Those of us who were underweight got to eat in a separate area about half an hour's walk from the rest of the group. The nurses in that area were caring, and the food, sweetened flat bread called 'papa' eaten with a chicken or beef stew, was better than any I had ever tasted.

Looking back, in some ways taking us to Itang was cruel, not because it was bad but because it did nothing to help us prepare ourselves for what was to come next.

By March 1988 we were finally taken to Pinyudo, where we would be put together with the rest of the children who were taken from different parts of Sudan and moulded into an army. It took us a week to walk from Itang to Pinyudo. My feet had begun to heal in Itang. Now came a new test: we were walking barefoot on a bitumen road, which was very hot, and the soil we walked on was coarser here, so my feet began breaking up again. Soon my blisters and cuts were burning with pain and I was straggling along like a cripple.

My first impression when we arrived at the Pinyudo camp was amazement: there were so many children. Most were thinner and younger than me, some with eyes bulging. It was a sea of little people; they were everywhere you looked. All up, more than 20,000 children had been brought here. They were all working, carrying firewood or doing other jobs such as building new houses, fixing houses that had fallen down, digging trenches, and fixing fences. It looked like a great big confusing workhouse.

Instantly I knew, no matter what had been said to us before, no matter how many good things we'd been told, that this was not right. I couldn't believe that this was what we had travelled all this way for. Afraid I would be separated from my cousins in this overcrowded place, I wanted to run back to Itang or, better still, all the way back to my village in Sudan.

As we marched through the gates of the camp I tried to take in as much as I could, but my mind felt as though it was racing to keep up with everything happening around me. There were so many people, it was hard to know where to look. Suddenly there was a lot of movement and one group began running after a boy, yelling that he was a thief. The thief, who was running so fast he could have been an athlete, looked as though he'd get away. He would wish that he had. As soon as he was caught he was dragged to the ground and the group who had been chasing him began bashing him, whilst others gathered round and cheered.

Around them, everyone else carried on as if nothing had happened. Children were carrying loads of firewood, some were standing on parade, others just looked lost.

I continued walking, pushed along by the shuffling feet behind me. As the newest group to enter the camp, we were the day's entertainment. Children and officers stared at us as we passed. I couldn't work out whether they were pleased to see us or if they resented our intrusion into what had become their home.

Around us was bare ground, with no trees except in the distance, and smoke rising from fires tended by children cooking maize and beans. It smelt as though the bush was on fire, the smell of the smoke just managing to overshadow the smell of human waste – not a pleasant combination!

I had expected some kind of formal parade of our own when we arrived, but instead we were herded quietly towards the dormitories, small rooms that slept up to thirty of us. They had mat walls, wooden frames and grass roofs. We would have to make our bedding. The other boys had tied together rectangles of sticks from the bush and covered them with grass as their 'mattresses'. As I looked inside the first dormitory we came to, I wondered how I would ever manage to sleep with so many others in one room. We weren't yet allowed to know which was our room – that would be decided later in the day. Everything now seemed quiet – I was resigned to this being my fate by now, and I just wanted to get on with it. The sooner I got through this, the sooner I could go back home.

My first impressions of Pinyudo shocked me. Everything was rough and ramshackle, and from the aggressive mood in the place it was clear that this was not a town with a school, this was another tough army situation. Immediately boys asked the sergeant about the schooling and food and friends we had been promised, but he would respond with harsh orders and arguments.

The silence was broken by groups of older boys coming around, ordering us to do things.

'Wash this, you're the newcomers – it's your job to do our work,' said one of them.

'You have to give us your clothes, you have to make a contribution,' said another.

As a new camp entrant you were able to 'choose' a set of clothes – a T-shirt and a pair of shorts that you had to pull out of a lucky-dip bag – but I ended up giving mine to these older boys. Giving clothes away seemed better than risking a bashing. This was a cycle that was repeated with each new group that entered the camp. We were simply the latest and easiest pickings. Later, we would be expected to take the clothes from the next group in.

When we had settled, the parade that I had expected earlier was organised. In total there were ninety of us new arrivals. We were broken into smaller groups of around thirty. This was the new *basila* that I would eat with, sleep with, train with and potentially fight with. None of my cousins was with me, something the army did intentionally. Some of the boys who had intimidated us earlier turned out to be in my *basila*. I figured I had already shown them the respect that they were after.

During the parade we were welcomed to the camp by a head teacher (who was also an SPLA officer) and told some of the basic rules. We would be banned from going to the Ethiopian shops, or associating with people outside our group. Some Sudanese women and children were living there, the wives and children of men who were fighting somewhere else. We couldn't mix with them, or with the Ethiopians who lived in Pinyudo. Military police controlled our movement, sitting on the fringes of the markets to make sure we didn't come in. Anyone who left without authorisation would be punished – without mercy. The punishment would involve beating, being put on cooking duty, cleaning dishes, having to get endless loads of firewood or being made to walk for hours to find water for the camp. Our drinking water was obtained either from the one tap in the camp, about thirty minutes' walk away, or from the river running alongside Pinyudo. The walk to the river took forty minutes, but at least there wasn't a long queue when we got there. We were not allowed to travel out of the camp, even if we were sick. Travel passes were needed before we were allowed to get medical treatment. If we got a travel pass we had to then walk more than ten kilometres to the Pinyudo hospital. Visiting friends in other *basila*s was not permitted unless we had special permission from our leaders. We were reminded that we were here to stay for as long as we were told. Beyond that, we had no idea what the future held.

With the rules clearly spelt out, we were given jobs to do around the camp. I was given the task of collecting firewood. From now on I would spend hours each and every day bringing in firewood from wherever I could find it in the forests around Pinyudo.

As I set about collecting my first bundle of firewood, I was able to have a proper look around. It seemed as though every-where I looked someone was cooking over a fire. I wondered if there would be any wood left for me to collect. Still as shy as ever, I found it hard to make conversation with strangers. Instead I chose simply to look and listen to find out information about my new home.

It became obvious to me that the camp was not just for the military. There were civilians here too. It was hard to tell the difference, though, because we were told not to wear uniform in the camp. I would learn later that this was because staff from the United Nations would often come to the camp to offer aid. Before Pinyudo, I knew next to nothing about the UN. In Pinyudo, all I was told was that they were people from other countries who brought us food and clothes, but if they saw us in our military uniform we wouldn't get anything, as they would see us as purely members of the army who, they believed, were part of the trouble. So the UN was, for me, not a place to go for help but a potential trap to work around.

Very few of us were allowed to speak to the white people in the camp anyway. Those who were allowed were told what to say. The army leaders had a knack of getting children who didn't speak any English to represent the rest of us. When the white people asked their questions the children answered freely, but the translations that were given were nothing like what they had really said.

The truth about Pinyudo quickly emerged. Pinyudo was the official, UN-backed refugee camp, and the SPLA wanted it to look like that, but the reality was that it was a military camp in all but name. The SPLA officers didn't show their guns or wear their uniforms, as the UN would not give food or shelter to men carrying guns. The SPLA built schools and the UN gave us pens and books and blackboards, but it was all part of the charade to trick the UN into giving us rations. Once we had our UN food in our hands, SPLA officers would come and requisition half, to send to frontline soldiers.

Two hours' walk from Pinyudo was Marakus, the real army camp that the UN didn't know about. This was where the SPLA stored their guns, uniforms, army transport vehicles and tanks. Here we would receive the harshest of our training, away from the prying eyes of the UN.

Marakus was an open place with some big mat-and-grass buildings in the middle of the bush.

I remember my first night there. In the dormitory buildings, wooden poles were dug into the ground, and bedding was stretched between these poles and set up like bunks. The first night was all right, and I kept to myself. In Pinyudo I had been disappointed and unhappy, and on my toes with the fights going on every day. It was a waste of time, all the pretending we had to do for the UN. I wanted to be trained properly, straight away, and given a gun so I could protect myself. I was impatient now to become a soldier.

In Marakus there was no laughing, there was no sickness, and we were on our best behaviour. If we complained, no one would listen to us. At best the officers in charge would make fun of us; at worst they would reward us with a heavy punishment. If they thought we needed it the leaders were also licensed to torture us at their will.

The military police did the punishing. The morning started with a whistle, and they would beat anyone who was not up and running fast to assembly to stand at attention. I had to race to get ahead of the next person so that he'd be punished instead of me. The typical punishment was thirty strokes of a stick, but they also made us stand with our arms spread and stones in our hands for a couple of hours. If our hands dropped, they beat us. Another punishment was to make us run to the river and jump in fully clothed, then beat us as we ran back, soaked. Or they would make us roll in the sand in wet clothes, and beat us if we refused. Or they'd bark orders: 'Stand up, sit down, stand up, sit down!' Or you would have to crouch-jump for two hundred metres. These punishments would happen every day, even for the most minor offences.

For three months we were taught how to handle attacks, how to defend, how to shoot and how to kill. We were given replica guns to train with and were told that it was our job to defend our country. The discipline that I had faced at home was nothing compared to the discipline dished out in the camp. They would make us stand in the sun with arms extended and a stone in each hand. They would make us collect water, carry it back in heavy buckets, then pour it out and go and get it again. Everything we did in training, they beat us with sticks while we were doing it. At least at home I knew that I might be beaten because my family wanted me to be respectable; here it was to put me in line and keep me there.

Apart from training us in combat, the military spent a lot of time manipulating us with stories to justify the fighting. Most of what they said, I had already heard from my father. They told us that Muslims came down to Sudan in the eighteenth century from the Arab world. They came as traders, and when they settled they began to force Africans to be Muslim. When the Sudanese refused and wanted to keep to their own cultural and religious backgrounds, the traders began to kill the locals and force others, including women like our mothers and sisters, and children like ourselves, into slavery. They told us about the extremes of sharia law enforced by the Muslims: if you stole, the Arabs cut your hand off. They told us that the Arabs had stolen our water from our rivers and exploited the oil that came from our land.

To make us angry, they told us that our families were now being killed by Muslims. Not having any contact with home, we couldn't tell if they were telling the truth or not, and many of us believed our families were dead. I believed them, and was distraught. I wanted to fight now. They said we needed to use our guns to defend our country or we would be pushed off the land. I thought back to the attack on my village the year before, and the near-death of my grandmother. What they were saying made sense to me.

Everything about Marakus was harsh. It was as if we were no longer human. Tuk tuk, a kind of foot rot, was everywhere. Your toes would itch and soon you would have an infection that could only be treated by putting your feet close to an open flame. We were working so hard, in unsanitary conditions, already weak and malnourished and boys got sick all the time. I was extremely lucky, as I never got badly sick. The soldiers didn't care if we were sick; in fact, if we were and we complained they would punish us. I remember one child making the fatal mistake of complaining to the corporal about feeling sick. The corporal passed the complaint on up the ranks, first to the sergeant and then to the senior trainer, who was not impressed. I remember him yelling out words to the effect of 'Bullshit'. Then he ordered the military police to rough the boy up. It was as if they were testing him to see how sick he really was, only they didn't care what the result was. In the end they beat him so badly that the boy begged to be killed. His final torture was the granting of his request – only they would not give him a quick death; instead they waited for his injuries to take their toll. Several hours later, he died.

His wasn't the last story like this. When other children 'died in training', the military covered it up by saying the child had simply been sent to another hospital. Those who had been witness to the truth were threatened with death themselves.

I would eventually witness the disappearance of many of those who had walked and trained and lived alongside me.

On the other hand, if you had genuinely committed a crime and were deemed deserving of death, you were put up as an example for all to see. The rest of us would be warned that we would be next. This was a threat that we took seriously.

The first time I saw someone being executed was in Pinyudo in 1989. We were back in the main camp and had been told the night before that the SPLA leader, John Garang, was going to be coming. Everyone was excited because to us at the time he was considered a hero. Every time the military leaders spoke, they would say something about what a great man John Garang was. They referred to him as 'The Chairman', or 'Doctor', or 'C-in-C' for 'Commander-in-Chief'. Even though I didn't know much about him, I held John Garang in great awe. Some nights they would play military music over loudspeakers: this meant either that the SPLA had captured a town or that John Garang was coming.

I was as excited as anybody else to see the fabled Garang. I didn't have negative feelings yet about the SPLA, even though life was so hard in Pinyudo and Marakus. The SPLA wasn't the bad guy in this war. The SPLA wasn't going into villages like mine and shooting people. The SPLA was protecting the southerners from Muslim militias. My father and two brothers had joined the SPLA, and I saw following them as my duty. I was training as a soldier – this was hard, and hateful, but necessary. I might have hated individuals who were cruel to us, but I had not yet turned against the SPLA.

I still hadn't seen Garang. Normally everyone would be up around 5 am, but this night I remember not being able to sleep amid all the singing and talking around camp. From about 3 am, people were starting to prepare for the arrival of our leader. By the time the sun rose, everyone was ready for our grand parade. A military car with a loud speaker was going through the camp instructing everyone to assemble in an area that was normally used as a kind of parade ground. Once we were all gathered, a commander addressed us. He told us the SPLA were winning the war, and our homeland Sudan was being reclaimed. The parade erupted in cheers. He continued, mentioning individual villages and towns that had been liberated. My village was never mentioned, and I still didn't know anything about what had happened there. As far as I knew, Baal and Panaruu had been captured and all my family incinerated.

The commander then announced that the Chairman was not coming to the camp. The disappointment instantly changed the atmosphere of the parade. He started to talk about the need for discipline and the respect for law within the camp. As he did this, two men and two boys were herded in front of us. They each had their hands tied, and one thick rope was tied around their legs, connecting them all. The two men were in their early twenties and the boys were roughly the same age as me. The commander's tone became harsh and he told us the men were accused of rape. A woman and her daughter had gone to the military police and accused the two men, who were brothers, of sexual assault. The younger two boys were said to have used their guns in order to steal and intimidate people within the camp. This, the commander said, would not be tolerated.

All four of them were petrified. The younger two were visibly shaking. Eleven soldiers then made their way across the front of the parade and lined up facing the prisoners. After a moment of silence the commander announced that all four would be put to death by firing squad. He called on the soldiers in the squad to draw their guns. Everyone in the camp was silent with fear. The two young boys had now wet themselves and were trembling uncontrollably, tears running down their faces. I couldn't help crying as I stood watching them about to die. The older two, stricken with fear, closed their eyes, flinching with each movement of the rope.

The commander gave the order for the soldiers to raise their guns, and shouted: 'Ready . . .'

Just as we thought they would fire, the two boys were cut free and ordered to move to the side. One of them couldn't walk, his legs having gone limp with fear. The boys were barely out of the way when the sound of AK-47s filled the air.

The two men lay lifeless on the ground. The parade, still silent, watched as the commander walked behind them and kicked them. He knew they were dead but as if to prove a point he drew a pistol, aimed at their faces and shot them again at close range.

By now I was shaking. I barely heard the commander speak as he ordered us all to file past the bodies and take note of what would happen to us if we chose to break the law. Within minutes everyone did as they were told. We were all made to look. As I went past I was horrified to see how the two men's bodies had been shredded and their faces torn apart. To this day, of all the guns I've heard, I can still hear those AK-47s and I can still see those two men as they fell to the ground.

It was through fear that they trained us to be able to keep secrets in case we were captured by government soldiers. For these exercises, we were split into two groups, one fighting the other. When we had captured our mock enemy we would interrogate them. If we were successful in getting information out of them, they would be in trouble – big time. Not only was the individual in trouble but the punishment would be extended to the rest of his group as well.

So, if in a real situation someone divulged information to the enemy, they knew what the consequences would be: the rest of the group would be killed by our own military police. It was better to be beaten to the point of exhaustion or even to sacrifice your own life than to risk the lives of all those around you. This was drummed into us: better lose my own life than be responsible for the loss of a hundred others.

There was one way of getting treated well in the camp: being good at sport. The UN would often come in and hold sporting events. These provided great photo opportunities so that the UN could look good to the rest of the world and people could say, 'What a great job they're doing – look how the children enjoy their sport!' Little was done to get to the truth behind the happy images, and the UN's photographers lapped it all up. If there was a soccer match, a volleyball game or a race of some kind, the winner would be celebrated by the leaders of the camp. The winners would get special privileges – for a short time they might even be treated as human beings.

This inspired me to play soccer, but unfortunately I was never picked on a team because I was too small. (I was always too small!) I watched as everyone around me got to have a go. I practised kicking a ball every night and during my spare time on the weekends, but no amount of practice was going to help me grow, and I would never make the team.

A grand final soccer match in the camp was something to see. I remember one particular game in the early evening when up to 10,000 people gathered to watch. Soccer was a distraction from the harsher realities. It provided us with something to smile about, something to cheer for. As the game got underway clouds of sand rose into the air, the crowd screamed and the tension in the camp was lifted. As each goal was scored the supporters started to sing and jeer the opposing team. One group sang out, 'Where are Group 12?' and another group sang back, 'Group 12 is in the pocket!' Translation – Group 12 has already lost!

There was always work to be done in the camp but for the duration of the match it was like a holiday – everyone was happy. That game was one of the few truly good memories I have of what should have been my childhood. Everyone cheered the final goal with what seemed like one last burst of happiness. The winners marched back to camp, singing and yelling all the way, imagining the glory of their prize, which might be extra clothes or a week of meat or light working duties, while the losers marched back as soldiers sinking back into the depression of camp life.

After the game was over we sat and ate what little food we had for that night. The food was never cooked properly and always had too much oil, water or salt. Many got diarrhoea and some of the children died as a result.

That night of the soccer final I remember eating the bean soup I had been given but thinking how bad it was. You couldn't refuse food or you would simply go hungry. That night the food was undercooked and smelt as though it had gone off. I gagged as I ate. Trying not to bring attention to myself, I forced the food down – a decision I would live to regret.

As the night dragged on I began to feel sick. At first it was my stomach. I felt as though I wanted to vomit, and eventually I did – throwing up so many times that I lost count. It was around midnight when the sickness suddenly became worse. I was now suffering from diarrhoea, I was sweating and I felt weak. In Sudan diarrhoea can be a matter of life and death. I knew boys who had died waiting for treatment. I became stressed just thinking about it. I also knew that the officers in the camp got angry at the children who were sick, as if it was somehow something we asked for or could control.

I struggled to my feet and tried to run the eight hundred metres from my shelter into the bush. I didn't make it. Instead

I made a mess of myself, dirtying the clothes I was wearing. I was drenched in diarrhoea. The smell was strong and awful. I was afraid it would attract animals from the bush. I imagined being attacked by a lion and being too weak to run or defend myself. This was not just a fantasy – many of the children went missing in the bush, never to be seen again. Lions were often seen around before or after the disappearances. Sometimes the children would be found half-eaten. As I thought about these things I began to realise that I was in danger. If I went back to the camp dirty I would be punished for sure. The longer I stayed in the bush, especially in the middle of the night, smelling as I did, the more likely I was to be the next child found half-eaten.

The diarrhoea continued, and I couldn't move. I collapsed, exhausted, in the bush. Suddenly I heard a noise. I couldn't tell if it was a pack of animals or people from the camp – it was hard to hear over my pounding heart. Weak and confused, I tried to pull my pants up. Diarrhoea still flowing, I stumbled as I tried to run. Behind me, the sound of dry grass crunching beneath heavy feet was growing louder by the second. I now heard voices and knew it was the officers from the camp. I heard the voices of some children too, shouting out directions for where they thought I was. I ran as fast as I could but I felt as though my legs were barely moving. The sound of their voices grew louder and meaner. Without warning I felt blow after blow around my head and body as the officers ordered the children to beat me.

I tried to yell and tell them how sick I was, but no one was listening. Instead of the other children going easy on me, it was as if they were taking out all of their frustrations on me instead. Tears began to flow down my face. I cried as I'd never cried before. How could those I had suffered alongside be so viciously attacking me? What had I done to deserve their hatred? I remember crying so hard and for so long that my tears eventually dried up, despite the agony continuing. The sound of their screaming voices seemed to drown into a high-pitched ringing as I felt each kick and thud pound me further into the ground.

Later I crawled back to clean myself up with some cold water and sleep with my platoon. The next day, tired and exhausted, I was paraded in front of the whole camp. I hadn't been allowed to change, and so by the time the sun had risen the smell coming from my body was unbearable. Flies were swarming around me. There were so many flies it was as if they had formed a new layer of skin over my body. All I could think of, though, was the reaction of the 1500 children who stood watching in silence. Among them were those who had spent the night torturing me. I wondered if any of them cared, if any of them felt anything at all now that they could see how helpless and weak I was. The humiliation was much worse than the physical pain.

Before my ordeal was over, I suffered another beating in front of the camp and was made to do push-ups until I could feel my body break. I had to listen to the entire camp sing, in military chorus: 'I will not shit close to my camp again.'

All this took place in the heat of the morning sun. I was so dehydrated I thought I would die. I wanted to die. I wanted my mother.

Finally, when they were done with humiliating me, they left me lying face-down in the dirt and moved off for their day's training.

What seemed like hours later, the nurses came and scraped me off the ground. I spent two weeks in the camp hospital – why, I wondered, would they now nurse me back to health? Were they not pleased with what a good job they had done at making me so sick?

But in its terrible way, this part of my training worked just as they intended. After I had recovered, I returned to my group, desperate to prove myself. Knowing how the officers didn't like children who were sick or complained, I was determined to show that my strength had returned and I was now strong enough to hold a gun.

It wasn't the first time I'd held a real AK-47 – I'd sometimes carried one at home to protect our cattle – but it was the first time I'd had a gun of my own and the first time I was expected to use it as a weapon of war. I felt proud. It was a symbol of maturity, or at least I thought it was. I felt that now I would be respected and no one would pick on me or beat me.

We were only allowed to use our guns in practice around the camp, aiming at targets to improve the accuracy of our shot. When we did other exercises such as running or planning for attacks, we would use wooden replica guns. This was to get us used to holding the guns in the right way and to having them with us wherever we went.

When we were old enough to hold a gun properly, we were considered ready to fight. Because I was still young and skinny, they kept me at the camp to fatten me up. I would have to wait for my time to come. The main reason I was not allowed to go and fight was that they didn't think I could carry an AK-47 and ammunition. They didn't know how old we were – we didn't even know – so we were assessed more by our size and strength. Some boys would stand on stones to seem taller. At my size I couldn't fool them, I was still too small. I was disappointed – I had come here to join the SPLA, to fight, yet it was beginning to seem that my future was to be a worker in the camp, to collect firewood and do the worst jobs for the others. It was going to be years before I grew big enough to be selected to go to the frontline. I wasn't a soldier but part of the army's backbone for a long war, and I hated that.

***

My cousins Wour and Ngor were lucky enough to be put in Group 11 together. I only got to see them on weekends, although I could call out to them in their barracks and we could have conversations. I needed permission from the officers to see them, but these attachments were discouraged, so I only saw them about once a month. They were struggling as much as I was. Bol and Mayer had gone to a place called Bilpam for training, instead of Pinyudo. I heard that they had moved back to Itang and were waiting to be sent home again to fight. My cousin Chol was somewhere in Pinyudo, but I could never find him. The army did everything they could to break these family ties. To this day I have never seen him again. Family members have told me that he is a radio operator in the Sudanese army.

In the camp we were given a basic education: taught our ABCs, how to write our names and how to do rudimentary maths. Our classes were divided the same way as our military training groups, so I was in Group 12 with thirty others.

In Group 12 I had one friend called Seji Cholgak, whom I'd known back in Panaruu. He had been in a different *basila* on the march, but we were in the same *basila* here in Ethiopia. We stayed close together. It was us two against everybody else, and we didn't trust anybody. We were both quiet and passive, and got pushed around by stronger boys.

This wasn't an environment where you were expanding your world – you just wanted to get through each day unharmed. I found boys from other tribes strange and frightening, and also other Dinka boys who spoke unfamiliar dialects, but I did my best to establish a name as someone not to mess with. There was a boy from the Nuer tribe called Duop, and he and I got in a fight. With Dinka, biting in a fight was seen as acceptable conduct, and as Duop wrestled me I planted a lot of bite marks on his arms. He and his Nuer friends left me alone after that – I had a reputation as a nasty biter, and that was okay by me.

On weekday mornings we would march to school singing political songs, praising our military high commanders and the success of the SPLA, while mocking or criticising the government. The schooling took place in buildings made of mud walls with wooden roofs held up by three big poles. There were no chairs, so everyone had to go to the forest to fetch a rock or a pile of mud to make a seat. The teachers used a blackboard and chalk, and we were allowed to take turns writing on the board. No electricity meant that every time it rained it grew so dark that we couldn't see the blackboard, so we stopped working.

Classes also took place outside in the open air, where we would copy out our dictation with our fingers in the dirt. It saved on exercise books. We did have two books, one for writing and one for maths. But we were not meant to waste a single line of paper. For every mistake we made, the teachers would hit us with a stick.

I hadn't been to school back in my village, so there were kids my age who had learned much more than I had. I was learning the equivalent of kindergarten, at the age of about twelve. It was discouraging to see others know so much more, but I was also afraid of getting beaten, so I struggled hard.

The typical school day would finish around 5 pm, but we would have to stay in class until 6 pm doing our homework. Then we would march back to camp, singing the same songs about the glory of the SPLA.

School at Pinyudo was compulsory even if you were sick. Only if you were on cooking duty, which included fetching water to drink, were you allowed to miss school. About ten children would do the chores for ninety others. We would only eat once a day, usually at night. To be honest, cooking duty was always more fun than school – at school we would be beaten for not counting or getting our alphabet right. When we did cooking duty, they left us alone.

Cooking duty also gave us a chance to enjoy the food, because we could cook it right. Food was our way of teaching other lessons that were more useful than school, such as 'Be good to me or I won't give you good food'.

School wasn't entirely bad. We learned some basic science, such as the parts of the human body. There was a little bit of Christian education from going to church on Sundays. We learned agriculture by planting and tending cabbage, tomatoes and onions in the school fields, a few hectares of land beside the classroom block. Tending the garden was almost as good as being on cooking duty. We would hide a small container of oil and some salt to take out, so that we could eat in the field. The soil was good and the tomatoes grew tall. But overall it was not a good way to learn. I wanted to go to Itang and learn – there was a private school system there, but of course I had no money and no freedom to go back there.

Only one boy in Pinyudo spoke English: Emmanuel Jel, who was in Group 9, He could communicate between the Sudanese and the UN. Later in life, he was taken to England and became a famous rapper.

Arabic was taught in the schools in Pinyudo: broken Arabic, not formal. They thought it would be good to learn the language of our enemies, and it was the official language of Sudan. A lot of the military language, in training, was also Arabic, or a variation of it. Arabic also helped you become a boss – you needed it if you wanted to be a leader.

Education was new to me, and I could see boys who were proud of what they had learnt. I had no school background from Panaruu, so I had to learn the hard way. At the beginning, a boy challenged me to write my name, and I couldn't. He teased me, so I told myself, 'I've really got to learn to write.' When I saw my name written by another boy, it looked cool – I said to myself, 'I have to do that.' Then, in our groups, there were competitive spelling games in which you lost points if you made mistakes. I loved to play these games and to win. There are many motives in the world to get yourself educated, and mine were not exactly ordinary. But they worked, and I was soon ambitious to learn more.

I spent two years in Ethiopia, which seemed to take forever. There was so much time devoted to training us to be ready to fight, yet nothing ever happened: we weren't fighting, and we weren't given leave. It seemed as though we were stuck in camp forever.

Finally I came to a decision: I had to go back to Sudan. I was tired of the camp. I wanted to defend my family and my village – it was what I was trained for, what I was waiting for. I didn't even know if my family were alive anymore, but I had to find out. What was the point in staying in Pinyudo forever? I hated it, and saw some of the worst things in my life there. I was afraid that in order to survive I would need to become as bad as some of the other people, who had learnt to do worse and worse things to get by. You always made enemies, people were always taking your possessions, and you had to defend yourself. If I stayed there, I knew that the need to survive would turn me into an animal. It took a long while to come to me that I had to leave, but once I decided, the need fell on me with full force. I had to leave right away. I could think of nothing else.

Looking back, I realise I had no idea what I was wishing for, nor any idea how soon my wishes would be turned into nightmares.

When it came down to it, leaving wasn't so hard. In the end I wondered why I hadn't tried to go earlier. I heard about a group who was being sent to a town called Nimule in southern Sudan, on the border with Uganda, to be trained as policemen and agricultural bosses. Every time the SPLA captured a new town, they would send men there to secure the place by acting as police and running the town's affairs. If the fighting returned to that town, these men would be converted back into soldiers. I asked if I could go with them. The military refused, so the day the group were due to leave, I took a can of water and another of maize meal and crept out of the camp. I hid in the bushes outside the perimeter. If the military couldn't find me, they couldn't stop me.

Finally the group came along; I stepped out of the bushes and showed myself to them. I gambled that they would not send me back, because it would delay their mission and they would lose one of their soldiers as my escort. My bet paid off. They decided it was easier to let me join them, and together we made the journey back to Sudan.

CHAPTER 3

Return to Sudan

SINCE I HAD BEEN IN ETHIOPIA, I had had no contact with my family. Any contact with Sudan had to take place through a military radio operator, and often it took more than two weeks to get the parties at both ends ready at the same time. On top of that, you would have needed your family to be near a radio in the first place – which wasn't the case with mine. And on top of that, you needed connections and influence in Pinyudo. I had none.

So I had no idea how my family were, or even where they were. I was desperate for news of them, but when I fled Pinyudo I also bore an amount of shame. When my elder brothers had come back home from the army, they had had their own guns. They had celebrated their return home by firing their guns into the air. As for me, I had only used a gun in training and didn't have one of my own. People would ask if I'd really been with the SPLA, or if I'd really been in Ethiopia at all. Monyleck would interrogate me and, after our history, I was scared of that. I thought he might even send me back to Pinyudo. Or, he would hold me up to ridicule for running away.

It was a hard place to be in for a boy of twelve, or thirteen, or however old I was. I wanted to see my family more than I wanted anything in the world; but it was a scene that I also feared more than anything in the world.

In any case, it was a lottery whether I would be going anywhere near my home. Once I fell in with the group, I had to go where they were going, and it turned out that they were going nowhere near Bentiu. Instead, they were going to Nimule in eastern Equatoria, south of where we were, close to the border with Uganda.

I trailed along at the back of the group for two months. I was the youngest, and the only one without a gun. Our progress was slow because wherever we found a village who would give us food, we would rest for a few days.

Villagers usually welcomed us, because they relied on the trade with army groups, who brought in clothes or medicine in exchange for food. I brought Panadol which I had taken from the clinic at Pinyudo, and it was good currency. We also gave them bullets, as they often had guns but no ammunition. Mostly the villagers supported the SPLA, except where groups had come through and stolen from them. If we went to the village leaders and asked for supplies, offering to trade goods rather than stealing from them, they were welcoming.

I had to carry whatever they told me to: a box of bullets, military equipment. All I possessed was the clothes I was wearing. I was able to fit in because I had learnt the one iron law of the SPLA: if you did what they told you, they left you alone. If you had a problem with taking orders, you attracted attention.

I did what I was told.

Then one day, as we made our way along the track, we began to notice the smell of a dead animal. The further we got the stronger the smell became. The air was thick with the smell and the humidity and there were vultures flying over us. We knew the animal was near. Some of the others tried to guess what it was, one suggesting a dead donkey and another thinking it was more of a fishy smell. Either way, it was bad and growing stronger by the minute.

Suddenly we heard gunfire in the distance. The sergeant yelled at us, 'Down, sit, sit, sit!' We crouched low as the sergeant listened intently to what was happening ahead. Whoever it was, they now seemed to be retreating and the gunfire had stopped.

Feeling more cautious now, the sergeant sent the landmine expert, a man named Okello, along the track ahead of the rest of us. Chances were that if there was fighting nearby there would also be landmines. Okello edged forward, watching each step, looking for changes to the surface of the ground, such as freshly turned soil or leaves in piles. For the most part the track had a smooth, hard-packed earth surface. It would be easy to see if any new mines had been planted. Okello didn't find any, but he did discover the dead animal. He stopped there, called us over and waited for us to pick over the remains with him.

It was not one but several animals, all lying there, some still in army uniform. Some had been stripped: their shoes, clothes, guns and ammunition all gone. There was one further into the bush who lay there, his hands up beside his face as if he were surrendering. His mouth and eyes were open, and bullet wounds covered his face and neck. As I looked I wondered if his family would be able to recognise him. Between the wounds, the swelling and the yellow discolouration of his skin, even those who knew him well would probably not be able to identify him now. I wondered also about his age. I think he would have been about seventeen or eighteen.

Nasir and Pinyudo had inured me to death and looking closely at dead bodies. I was no longer rigid with shock. When they'd executed those men in Pinyudo and made us march close past them, forcing us to look right into their faces, they had been preparing us for moments like this.

As I sat thinking about his family and what his life might have been like, one of the officers reached over and removed the gun and ammunition from him – he wouldn't be needing it any more. The officer then gave it to me. I accepted it, to protect myself.

We rejoined the rest of the group who had managed to pick over the other bodies – removing shoes, uniforms, whatever they could find. We hadn't been the first to find these dead soldiers, and whoever had been here before us were either low in numbers or had been scared off before they could take full advantage of what was left behind.

It felt wrong to be stealing from the dead, but we needed their supplies. If we didn't take them, someone else would. If it was a gun or ammunition that was taken, better we have it than it landing in the hands of our enemy.

We walked for two months south-west from the Ethiopian border. My legs were longer than when I'd covered the same distance in the opposite direction! At times we were ambushed by the Sudanese government army. The leaders of our group were shot at, and the rest of us dived for cover until it was over. These were minor skirmishes, but the war itself was now big, much bigger than I was prepared for and much bigger than when I had left Sudan. A lot of people had been and were being killed. Guns were everywhere, and villages had been either destroyed or abandoned after combat. The nature of the war seemed to have changed, too. Instead of it being the SPLA fighting the government, now the government-sponsored militias had broken up into factions, and so had the SPLA. The rebel army was in a general retreat towards the south. Civilians were armed now, and there was chaos everywhere, every village for itself, with no structure of support from either the government or the SPLA. I couldn't see how my family and village could have survived this.

After two months, in what must have been the middle of 1990, we arrived at our destination, the town called Nimule. The journey had been long, tiring and full of sights and sounds that I will never forget. I was tired of walking and being scared of every footstep due to the landmines that riddled the ground. By now I had lost any ounce of childhood. I wasn't the boy who had left Panaruu. I wasn't myself anymore. I had no sense of home and I felt no love. The army had moulded me into a hard, emotionless machine.

As we got closer to Nimule in the south, the SPLA presence grew stronger. Since I had left Ethiopia, a civil war had broken out there. The Ethiopian government was no longer protecting the SPLA, so the entire rebel army was converging on its only stronghold, south near the border with Uganda.

Nimule was a small town of about 40,000 people on a hill overlooking the Nile. The group I had walked with helped guard the town and trained as police and agricultural organisers. I started to go to school in a Catholic mission, run by the Diocese of Torit under Archbishop Taban. It was a big mission and included sisters from America, France, Uganda and Italy.

When we arrived in Nimule, the SPLA allowed me to go to school during the day and come back to the barracks at night. But once I was in the mission, I explained to the sisters that I wanted to leave the army as they weren't looking after me. I told them I was on my own and had no family. Taking pity on me, the sisters said I could live in the compound and move into the church and work there. It was a risk for them, but the

SPLA was weak and disorganised, with desertions taking place everywhere. If they captured me they still wouldn't send me to fight, as I was too small, but instead put me in a town, maybe at a machine gun post, to guard it.

I didn't want anything to do with the SPLA any more. I was tired, the army had ruined my life, it had lied to me, and I decided I had to get away from the war. Some other boys came into the mission with me to hide from the SPLA.

The mission consisted of a group of well-built concrete structures with electric light and high ceilings. The floors were concrete and the beds were real. The sisters cultivated their own food, fed us and gave us shelter and clothes, and treated us if we were sick. This was a brief but happy respite for me – I was clean and well fed for the first time in months. I established good relationships with the sisters, who took responsibility for us like 'mothers', each with a few boys to look after.

This was the closest I had come to feeling happy since I had left my village. Right now, the sisters were the nearest thing I had to family.

While I stayed in the mission, the war was changing rapidly. Colonel Bashir had come to power in Khartoum in a military coup, strengthening the government push into the south. The weakened SPLA had destroyed the bridges and road entries to Nimule, so the government would bomb the town from air force Antonovs. At first it was just early in the morning and in the evening, but within months the bombings intensified, continuing all through the day.

I could feel every nerve in my body becoming metallic with fear as I heard the planes approaching. Their bombing runs would start at seven in the morning and continue until three or four in the afternoon. All the shops were forced to close and people couldn't get food. We would spend most of the day in a *khandag*, or bomb shelter. In our shelter we had seven people. It was hot as hell inside, and sometimes it would rain. Although some *khandags* had roofs to protect from the sun and the rain, many did not. At worst they were a hole in the ground designed only to stop you from being hit by shrapnel flying sideways after a bomb had dropped. If the bomb hit over the hole, you were dead.

My *khandag* had just branches and sand laid over it for a roof. Thirty to forty bombs a day would explode around me, and I became more and more nervous and scared. It's the worst kind of killing when you can't see the person who's trying to kill you. You live in a state of pure terror.

In a *khandag* in a nearby village, fifteen people died. I lost my best friend at the time, whose name was David Kiir. I had only met him in Nimule, and we had sat in classes together. We played soccer together and fished and swam in the Nile. He was in love with guns, and attended school less than I did. When we had problems, I usually suggested we go to the sisters, but David would say, 'If we go to the sisters, we are like civilians.' He saw himself as a soldier, a warrior. He died a warrior's death.

In the breaks between the bombings, life in the Nimule mission had its benefits. We had beds, clean water and healthy food. On the other side of the coin, we had little contact with the outside world, little protection from the bombs and little hope of a life that was free from the worries that burdened us all. Hope, to me, was the most precious thing in life – while ever there was hope there was a future. Under the guidance of the sisters, I made it a point to always carry a little bit of hope with me wherever I went.

But this hope was rocked one day. An army group came through from my area, and everyone rushed out to ask for news. Wour – who had followed me from Pinyudo when the Ethiopian civil war started – and I found a soldier from Panaruu and asked him for news of our families. He looked at me and said, 'Your family are all right except for your sister Ajok.' I can't remember exactly what he said next – his voice seemed to be coming to me from a long, blurry distance – but the news was that my eldest sister had died of *kalazar* (bilharzia), a fatal parasitic disease common in southern Sudan. I was too shocked to ask for more details. Also, I didn't want to believe any more until I had spoken to my immediate family. I think this might have been my way of protecting myself from the pain: I wouldn't believe Ajok was dead until it was confirmed by the family I could find no way of speaking to.

The Catholic mission was full of fences. There was one large wire-mesh fence that surrounded the compound, a thatched-grass fence that separated the boys' areas from the girls', a fence surrounding the hospital and another for the leader of the camp, Father Leo. His fence was rarely crossed. His house was the most impressive of all the accommodation on site. The walls were brick and the floor concrete, although the roof was more traditional, made of thatched grass. Father Leo had his own generator, so he had electric light and refrigeration.

Father Leo was a grumpy old man, but he was fair in his treatment of us. I think he was Italian, but he spoke in English, his second language. He also knew enough Arabic to tell us when he was unhappy with us. My colloquial Arabic had improved with use in Pinyudo, and I certainly understood when Father Leo was cranky. He smoked a large black pipe which seemed to hang from his face like a surgically attached hook.

Among the jobs that I had in the camp was filling up Father's water tank. The corrugated-zinc tank was the tallest structure in the compound, towering over his house. There was a ladder leaning against the side of the tank, which I would climb, thirty-litre jerry can in one hand, the other hand holding on tight as I reached the top of the tank.

I shared the job with my friend Angelo Kuot. We were in the same class in Nimule. He had arrived there before me, but while I slept at the mission, Kuot slept in the military barracks. Kuot was from Bhar-el-Ghazal, west of where I grew up. He was taken to Ethiopia like me, and came down to Nimule when the Ethiopian war broke out. We had never met in Pinyudo, but we had a lot in common. He was the same age as me, and his father was also in the army. Like me, he was uncertain about what had happened to his family. He was luckier than me in one way: his brother Garang had been with him all the way and was still with him now. Angelo was taller and skinnier than me, and much more talkative! He laughed so much at times, he would fall over on the ground, attacked by his own laughter. He always wanted to look flashy: if anyone appeared wearing new clothes, Kuot would vanish, then reappear wearing something even better, even newer. He liked fooling around and would talk to anybody. I liked the way Kuot always talked up his big plans: 'Let's go to Uganda!' 'Let's go to Europe!' 'Let's run away and just travel together!' But he was still serious: he got mad with himself if he got a maths problem wrong, and he hated getting beaten for making a mistake. He was also good at talking his way out of trouble. He was an excellent shot, and we liked to hunt animals together, sometimes shooting a gazelle and selling the meat. His brother Garang wasn't anywhere near as friendly, and Kuot and I would gang up on him. The friction between the two brothers brought me and Kuot closer together.

He and I would take turns holding the bottom of the ladder as the other carried yet another jerry can of water to fill the tank. It would take fifteen to twenty jerry cans each time.

Filling Father Leo's tank was the most important job Kuot and I had to do all week. One day there was a soccer tournament in Nimule between army guys and the schoolboys. Everyone from the school was there to watch. The field wasn't very good – it was just a big patch of long grass cut with scythes – and no one had any boots or proper uniforms, but the tournament final was one of the most exciting I'd ever seen. Kuot and I were so wrapped up in watching the game that we completely forgot about filling Father's tank. Suddenly we heard an angry shout from the other side of the compound. It was Father Leo. 'Where's my water, where's my water?' The tank had had enough water for about thirty seconds of showering, and then it had run out. Kuot and I had about thirty seconds to race and fill the tank with enough water for Father Leo to finish his shower, otherwise we would be in serious trouble. We'd never been on his bad side before and didn't know what to expect. He was still yelling as we scrambled to the top of the tank with what water we could carry in one quick trip.

Expecting him to punish us, we were taken by surprise when he started to laugh as the water poured through to the showerhead.

'Don't forget my water again!' he laughed.

I didn't mind such a mild warning and it was the last time Father Leo had to wait for his shower to be filled.

Alongside Father Leo, the sisters taught us and looked after us in the mission. The two I had the most to do with were Sister Rita and Sister Shaun. Both were short and stocky, dressed in traditional habits, and both were Ugandans. The similarities ended there. Sister Rita was grumpier than Father Leo and twice as quick to anger. She would only give you biscuits, clothes or soap if you had worked yourself to a standstill. Sister Shaun was one of the gentlest human beings I'd ever met. If you were upset, she would listen carefully to your problem and wrap you in a giant cuddle as though she was your own mother. So we avoided Sister Rita when we could and gravitated to Sister Shaun. Unfortunately, there was a lot of competition for her!

I stayed in Nimule until I was about fifteen years old. I had fallen in love with the way the sisters lived: they were clean, they dressed neatly, they were kind (Sister Shaun, anyway), and they placed a lot of value on education. I had given up all hope of returning to my village by now. I wanted to be somewhere different, somewhere I could improve myself and live like the sisters.

When I was about fourteen, I received what I took as another sign to give up on going home. My cousin Wour, who was related to me on my blind grandmother's side, would go to the army radio station in Nimule from time to time and try to connect with someone back home. If the army had an outpost near the villages, they would have a radio. One day he managed to make contact, but he brought back terrible news. During an attack on our village by Arab militia, everyone had fled except for my grandmother. It had been hard enough getting her, with her walking stick, away from these attacks years earlier when I had been a child. Now she was older and weaker, and during this particular raid she had said to my mother, 'You go ahead, I cannot run with you, I will stay in the hut.' She surrendered herself to the mercy of the mujahideen. It was a fatal gamble. They burnt down the village, Wour told me, including the hut with my grandmother in it. She was dead. Having survived through these attacks myself, having left Grandmother in the long grass that memorable day, I could picture all too clearly how it had happened. I was more upset by my grandmother's death than by Ajok's. When I had been in trouble as a child, I always ran to Grandmother. She was kind and gentle with me, even more so than my own mother, who punished us because she feared my father. Grandmother never feared him – he was her own son! So when he wanted to punish me and I sheltered behind Grandmother, she waved her stick at him to keep him back. Even without her eyesight, she knew where he was!

Now I was more angry than ever – at my father, but mostly at the Arab government and their militias. Why did they have to burn down grass huts and kill blind old ladies? What threat did she ever pose to them?

Perhaps my indoctrination at Pinyudo and Marakus was meant to kick in now, and make the death of my grandmother spur me to rejoin the army. But I was changed now, I was growing up, and I had never been a natural soldier. I didn't rush off to find the nearest SPLA unit. Instead I buried my anger inside myself. I didn't show my feelings to anyone, not even Wour. All I thought was that I had to keep going forward and get out of Nimule.

In early 1993, Nimule started to be bombed again by the Sudanese government, a new escalation in the overall bombing campaign that went from 1990 to 1995. There was a bridge outside Nimule which was bombed, cutting us off. Within days, the bombings intensified, as if they were trying to wipe us out altogether. Still, Nimule was well guarded by the SPLA and the government infantry didn't actually try to invade. They just wanted to make our lives unbearable. Father Leo and the sisters soon began to pack up the mission in case they had to leave in a hurry. Up to thirty bombs a day were falling around the mission, and I could see that, as foreigners, they were beginning to think that the risk to their lives was becoming too high. We were lucky that none of the bombs fell within the church compound, but it always felt as though it was only a matter of time before we would be hit.

The tension never stopped. We would hear the hum of the plane before the bombs came, and when the bombs were being dropped, we wouldn't know where they'd fall. The plane being overhead didn't mean we were where the bombs would fall, and the plane having moved on didn't mean we were safe. The explosions would deafen us for fifteen or thirty minutes afterwards. I slept normally, but was always half-ready for aeroplane noise. Even when humanitarian planes came from the UN, people would run everywhere. I adjusted to it, but was always on my toes. The sisters put tarpaulins over their house with grass over the top of it to hide their roof, but that was all they could do other than pray.

Father Leo suggested that we go to Uganda to seek assistance from the Catholic Church there. The mission's territory straddled the border, so we hoped it would be just like Nimule but without the bombing. We held high hopes for Uganda. Even though it was only a few kilometres away, on the other side of a simple bridge, it seemed like a promised land.

For Father and the sisters, crossing the border in to Uganda would be possible, but for us Sudanese boys living with them, leaving Nimule would be extremely difficult. The SPLA were all around the mission and the town, and they would want us to fight with them, not go to Uganda. When I had left Pinyudo, I had been impatient to fight. But the school and the sisters in Nimule had changed me. Now, education was everything to me. I thought back to our family life, and how I had never been to school, and how education was held in low regard. In my mind, it seemed that all of our problems – as a family, as a tribe, as a people – resulted from not being educated. I had heard that John Garang's children, and the children of the other SPLA leaders, had been sent to school in countries like Cuba. We asked ourselves: if the point of our life is to fight a war to defend our country, why are our leaders' children, boys the same age as us, spending all their time in schools overseas?

Father Leo and his superiors gave us – myself, Kuot, Garang, Wour and two other boys – the message that they would help to get us to Uganda. We were the only boys in the mission then, and Father Leo and the sisters felt obliged to protect us, so they said they would send us ahead of them to Uganda. I waited as patiently as I could for this promise to become a reality, but the reality never seemed to eventuate. With the bombings growing worse than ever and the delays getting the better of us, we six boys got together and decided to make the journey on our own. We thought that in Uganda we would be safe. I thought I could continue my education and life might improve.

I didn't know it, but I was about to leave my homeland for the last time.

CHAPTER 4

Uganda

SIX OF US LEFT THE MISSION TOGETHER: Angelo Kuot, his brother Garang, Thomas Wour Kuol, Kuot's friend Matouh, a boy named James Arop, and me. We left on market day – the day the markets were held in Uganda. A lot of people were allowed to walk the three hours from Nimule across the border into Uganda on market day, to buy and sell food and other goods.

The church had packed our meagre possessions into bags and taken them ahead. As we walked, we talked constantly about the new life we imagined for ourselves in Uganda. We talked it up into a utopia: a land where the clamour of guns, bombs and screaming people would be replaced with the gentle sounds of birds singing and wind blowing through savannah grasslands.

I felt as though the war had taken a great toll on me. I felt like an old man, worn down by the life that had been handed to me since I had left my village. Already I had experienced what men twice or three times my age should not have had to endure. The weight of all my memories wearied me, like a heavy blanket over my head and shoulders, hampering my ability to move, to think, to stay alert. Yet I needed these faculties in order to stay alive. I was about sixteen years old now, and this was to be a most dangerous time.

As we had no goods to sell, and no adults accompanying us, and no papers, we couldn't pass through the official border crossing on the bridge. It would be obvious that we were trying to try to escape permanently to the other side. There were people smugglers you could pay on both sides of the border, but we didn't have enough money. We knew that there would be SPLA soldiers, complete with guns, on the Sudanese side, and on the Ugandan side there would be government soldiers in full military uniform.

So we decided that to be safe we had to walk fifteen kilometres – all of us in bare feet – to find an unpatrolled place to cross.

We planned to cross the river, a tributary of the Albert Nile, that divided Sudan and Uganda at Nimule. When we arrived at a narrow point in the river, even though it was only about fifty metres across we could see how difficult the crossing would be, due to the strong current and the thick bamboo and reeds that grew from its banks, not to mention the tsetse flies buzzing everywhere and the crocodiles that infested the waters. But we were also paranoid about the SPLA, waiting for someone to sneak up behind us and interrogate us. As much as the river scared us, staying in Sudan scared us more.

As we entered the water and found that it was rising to our chests, we realised there was another complication – only two of us, Angelo and I, could swim.

Thank goodness for all those days in my childhood when I had learnt to swim in the River Nile. I could do freestyle, back-stroke, breaststroke – we had spent a lot of time swimming to the little islands in the middle of the river to join the fishermen who were eating. I was one of the better swimmers in my village.

The water was deeper than we first thought and the current was stronger. Thinking quickly, we sent Angelo to the other side with a long rope, which he tied to a tree. We tied the other end to a tree on our side. One by one, clinging desperately to the rope, we all made it safely to the other side – to Uganda.

After we crossed, we were making our way through a banana plantation, which was also thick with pawpaw trees and bamboo, when we were attacked by bees. Arop and Wour went to cut down some bananas and accidentally cut down a bee hive. We all ran in different directions, some back towards the water, some into the bush. Twenty minutes later, the bees all seemed to have disappeared and we came back together to compare stings. Wour's whole body was covered in stings, and some of the others had badly stung faces. I got a few stings on my arms and torso. They hurt big-time and swelled up, but nothing as bad as Wour, whose whole face swelled up painfully. Angelo was laughing.

We would have to walk another twenty-four hours into Uganda to the town where we had been told the church was. It was very green, with villages farming sugar cane, maize, potatoes, tomatoes, bananas and mangoes. As it was the rainy season, it was very humid and tiring. One thing I noticed was how there was no UN presence: Uganda, being relatively peaceful, was not reliant on the UN as Ethiopia had been.

As we made our way deeper into Ugandan territory, worrying about being arrested, we tried to fit in with the people we came across. It was almost impossible. We looked like refugees: our bodies had become thin as rails, and we looked and felt as tired as elderly men. Yet instead of people taking pity on us on those rural dirt roads, they more often targeted us.

The biggest threat was the Ugandan rebels, the Lord's Resistance Army (LRA), who were hiding in the bushes every-where, waiting to leap out and rob people coming to and from the markets. The LRA, we heard, would steal the goods, shoot and kill the men and sometimes rape the women. The LRA was a separatist guerrilla movement in northern Uganda, and their conflict was not with us but with the government in the Ugandan capital, Kampala. But we Sudanese were fair targets if we came into their sights. When they wanted to rob civilians, they didn't discriminate. They came up to us in disguise, wearing the SPLA uniform. They chatted in a friendly way with us, speaking our language and talking about shared tribal history. Then they pulled their guns and told us to give them our money.

Thankfully, though, they weren't thorough in their robbery. Some of us had managed to hide money in our clothes, and when we made our way up to the main road we were able to buy some sugar cane from a roadside stall. Eventually we arrived at an open market. There were people lined up for all different kinds of goods: lines for dried fish, clothes, vegetables and even some lines for accommodation. Each of us lined up for our choice of food. I chose fish. I stood in line for about twenty minutes, ordered my fish and waited another ten minutes to eat it. It tasted good, and had become cheaper because by now it was about 3 pm and the markets would close at 4 pm. We bought some extra to take with us. I lined up for sweet potato and mangoes to eat along the way. Our plan was to walk now until six the following morning.

There was a moon casting enough light to see. As we walked along the road, traffic would come and we'd jump into the bushes to hide. We were also scared of wild animals in the bushes, but getting caught by soldiers or police was a bigger threat. Along the way we became separated several times. Some of us stopped because we were tired, while the others had enough energy to carry on. Then the leading group would stop and the slower ones would catch up. Halfway through the night we came to a small village. We could hear talking in the distance. They were speaking the language of the Acholi people, supporters of the LRA and tribal enemies of the Dinka. The Acholi blamed the Dinka for the war in Sudan, because John Garang was Dinka, and the SPLA was so closely identified with him. The Acholi perceived the war as a tribal conflict between the Dinka and the Arabs. So we, in turn, were taught to mistrust the Acholi.

When we heard these men speaking, we were frightened that they were LRA guerrillas. Kuot, Garang and Matouh spoke fluent Acholi but Matouh's bottom teeth had been removed, a Dinka tradition, which was a sure givaway.

Suddenly a soldier surged at us from the bushes, yelling in Acholi. We all ran in fright, dispersing into the bushes and running until we lost him. After scattering into the bush on both sides of the road, once the soldiers had passed, we continued walking in the same direction, not on the road but beside it. I met up with one and then two of the others. On the far side of the road the other three were doing the same thing. We walked in the bush beside the road like this for two hours before hearing each other's voices and meeting up. This was how we found each other again.

We arrived at the Catholic mission, at a place called Kichwa, at night-time. Kichwa, which was a seminary, was a part of the Torit Diocese and was connected to the mission we had left in Nimule. Our instincts told us that the missions were safe havens. Sister Shaun and Sister Rita had come here ahead of us, with our clothes and some food. Having escaped the bombing across the border, Sister Sophia was going to work here as an administrator.

We sat under a tree and it was lovely to see Sister Sophia. But her initial warmth wasn't a sign of things to come. When we first arrived under the tree, the sisters came to us with some maize and beans, but even though we were the only people sleeping outside, it was immediately apparent that there wasn't enough for the six of us. We took this as a signal that we weren't welcome to stay. Our relationship with the sisters seemed suddenly to have changed since Nimule. They had looked after us in Sudan, but now, when we were more helpless than ever, in a foreign country, they didn't seem to want to know us. We thought they had limitless goodwill and resources, and, because of their faith, they were going to solve all of our problems. Faith had its limits, clearly. It wasn't their fault that they disappointed us. It was that our expectations were too high. We'd thought they would always be our saviours. We'd thought they were perfect, because they were close to God, but clearly they were human, like the rest of us.

We weren't given accommodation inside the mission buildings, so we slept outside. When it rained we would shift our belongings onto a veranda. It was obvious that we were only allowed to stay here temporarily until they could find us a space in a refugee camp.

We thought we were guaranteed help at Kichwa, but eventually we were turned away. A watchman was called to get us off the property. But we hadn't come this far to give up easily. Instead of leaving as we were told, we decided to stay and sleep on the termite-infested grass outside the church doors.

After a long time of pleading and waiting, the bishop finally came to see us. He told us he would send us to a camp, Allara, that was holding more than 30,000 refugees. We had heard about Allara, and knew that many of the tribespeople there were enemies of the Dinka and might not welcome us. We told the bishop of our concerns, but he didn't seem to listen or care. He told us that the only other alternative was to return to Sudan, which we knew we couldn't do.

Unable to stay or go, we decided to make some kind of protest. We started a four-day hunger strike, which we spent praying in front of the bishop's church. We prayed loudly and constantly, hoping that the bishop would return with a changed mind and a desire to help us. We still ate a little bit, a few biscuits in our pockets, so that we could make our point without suffering too much!

He didn't. Nor did the sisters, who weren't available when we needed them most. After being hopeful for the first day or so, we became extremely angry and began muttering how the sisters were hypocrites. There were so many contradictions in the Bible, and this behaviour embodied them – how could they be so generous one day and so mean the next? We were angry, but we were terribly confused.

The four days came and went; eventually we gave up and accepted that we had to move on to the transit camp at Allara.

A white engineer drove us in his Land Cruiser. He was a quiet man, but it was all very exciting to us. We all fought over who got the front seat. Kuot eventually won. The engineer just smiled quietly. We gave in to our instinct for hope. I had been in cars a few times in Nimule and in a truck in Pinyudo, but this was the first time sitting with my friends, talking, happy together, in a nice car, going to a better place.

Allara was a UN camp, but the UN officials didn't sleep there. They slept in the neighbouring town of Par Kela.

As we pulled up outside Allara we saw about forty people rush towards the Land Cruiser. The engineer got out and started talking to the head of the camp. As they conferred, a crowd of people surrounded the car. They were talking in the Acholi language. They were saying that we had nice clothes and nice bags – but not in a nice way. Kuot, Matouh and Garang could hear them saying they were going to rob us as soon as we got out of the car. The engineer assured us that we would be okay, but we pleaded with him not to leave us there.

By now people were reaching into the car, wrenching the windows open, literally trying to pull the clothes off our back. The engineer, finally seeing the danger of the situation, started the car and began to pull away. As he did, the crowd started to throw rocks at us.

He decided to take us to Ogujebe, a much larger camp of tens of thousands of refugees. We knew that we would face the same situation as at Allara, but worse, given the size of Ogujebe. The houses were made of brick, one storey, with grass or zinc roofs, standing out amid thousands and thousands of white canvas tents. The River Nile ran alongside the camp, with some cultivation between the tents and the riverbank. There were no trees at all.

In the camp we were taken to a big reception room for new arrivals. There was a black woman there who spoke fluent Arabic. She was welcoming and wanted to know all about us. She asked about our families and seemed genuinely upset when we told her that none of us had our parents with us. She understood our story and kept repeating the words, 'We are all the same, we all the same.'

As a way of showing our appreciation, we gave her some biscuits to give to her own family, who were inside the camp.

Despite the warm welcome, we were wary of just how welcome we would be in the rest of the camp. We agreed amongst ourselves that Kuot, Garang and Matouh would not speak Acholi, as the members of the camp would then know that we understood what they were saying. We had to act like spies: we would speak only Dinka. This proved more than helpful, as later that night Kuot overheard people talking about us in Acholi. It was not good. To our face they spoke of how they would help us find fellow Dinka and Nuer tribespeople in the camp, but behind our backs they spoke of how they would murder us and take our belongings.

We huddled together, unable to go to sleep, watching nervously while Kuot went looking for friendlier people. Eventually he came back, saying he had found seven Nuer we could trust. So we picked up our belongings, watching the Acholi people warily, and went off to stay in a hut where the Nuer were living.

They hosted us for two weeks. We sent Kuot back to the mission at Kichwa to tell them what had happened and to ask for money for a house that was being built next to the Ogujebe compound. The Acholi, who had been there the longest and were the ones doing the building, were offering the house for sale at twenty-five thousand Ugandan shillings. It was a lot of money: we could work for two years and not save anywhere near that much. We had nothing, but we saw the promise of this house as a base we could establish, to build up some kind of security for ourselves.

Kuot exploited the sisters' feeling of guilt for having turned us away. He told them that if we couldn't have the house, we would all show up back in Kichwa and make pests of ourselves again. The sisters gave him the money to pay for it, but they, not we, became its owners. Kuot promised that we would be self-sufficient and not ask them for another thing.

It was in Ogujebe that I registered with the United Nations as a refugee. Life was a little bit better, as I was getting food rations from the UN, which consisted of a little bag of beans, lentils, salt and oil handed to us every fifteen days, and no one was bombing me. I had shelter, and could return to school. I remember smiling for the first time in a long time, but then remembering that I didn't know where my mother, father or any of the surviving members of my family were. If there were any survivors at all. My smile faded.

***

As much as we were happy to have our own house, it didn't take long for things to fall apart. We quickly found ourselves under financial stress. The UN food rations were too scant to go around, so we needed to trade things like salt and oil for meat, onion and fish. You could trade at the markets in Ogujebe where people would come in with fish and better food. But being new arrivals and young, we were right down the bottom of the system and had little of value to trade. I wanted to go to school, so there was also the matter of finding money for textbooks, materials and fees amounting to hundreds of Ugandan shillings. In time we had to sell almost everything we had. These pressures broke up our group: Kuot, his brother Garang and Matouh thought that things could be no worse back in Sudan, so they left. There were four of us left in the house: myself, Wour, Arop, and a guy called Samuel Dut who had followed us from Nimule. Now that the church had bought us the house, they were directing new boys from Sudan to come here. Samuel, whose English was fluent and who wanted to be a priest, would be followed by several more.

I stayed behind because I wanted to study, and because I had nothing to go back to in Sudan. There was a flood of Sudanese leaving Nimule to come to Uganda. The SPLA, trying to stop this, were capturing boys and taking them back to the frontline north of Nimule.

I felt sad saying goodbye to Kuot, but was sure I would see him again. We didn't make a big deal of the farewell: I was already torn between going and staying, and didn't want my friendship with Kuot to sway me to change my decision. So we made it a light-hearted, casual 'see you later'.

Despite having said goodbye to Kuot, I remembered my resolution to keep some germ of hope in my heart, and I placed that hope in the education I could get in Ogujebe. At last, with the war and the SPLA behind me, I thought I could concentrate on my studies. To me Uganda was a promising part of the world, relatively peaceful and totally different from my village in Panaruu. I longed to find some kind of happiness, and thought that it was now time for me to put my bad memories to rest and search for knowledge.

The school, built by the UN, had more than two thousand kids in it. The classes each had forty to fifty children of all ages and standards, lasting from morning to late afternoon, five days a week. Mostly the teachers were Ugandan and were barely more advanced in their education than ourselves. But it was an organised education at least, and I grew cautiously optimistic about my future.

Just as life seemed to make sense and I started to feel some kind of security, I got an unexpected visit from Atem, who had been one of my friends back in Pinyudo. He had made contact with the mission in Nimule and the sisters had told him that I was now in Ogujebe. He was one of the boys they sent after us.

He arrived one evening with a letter from my uncle Dongwe, one of my father's half-brothers. Atem told me that I had just missed my father, who had come to Nimule for a meeting of elders a short time after I had left for Uganda.

After I had welcomed him, Atem said, 'I have a letter for you.' He reached into his bag and handed me a white envelope with a red and blue airmail border.

Letters were not generally a good sign for me. After receiving such bad news the year before about the deaths of my sister and my grandmother, it now scared me to open the envelope. What if this letter brought more bad news from home? My hand started to tremble and I could feel my stomach tying into knots. Putting the envelope down again, I tried to make myself relax. This could be good news, I told myself, good news about my friends in Nimule.

I picked the envelope up again and tore it open. The letter, on a single sheet, was handwritten by some scribe at Dongwe's dictation – I knew my uncle couldn't have written it himself, as he was illiterate. I started to read. It was all right! My fears were for nothing. Atem's letter was harmless. There was news about Nimule and the mission and what various people had been doing. Feeling relieved, I read on. By the time I got to the last paragraph I was completely calm. Then I got to the point of the letter, which lay concealed like a lion in long grass waiting for its moment to pounce.

My uncle simply wrote: *Chol I am sorry to say this but I have bad news for you – your mother is dead*.

There was no explanation, not one more word.

I refused to believe it. This would not be the first time I had heard a false rumour about one of my family dying. My brother Monyleck, I thought, he has been killed many times! But now, even though he has been in many dangerous situations, he is alive and looking after my poor sister Ajok's three orphans!

I kept saying to myself: I know in my heart that my mother cannot be dead. I will go back and see her. I remembered her last words to me, calling me 'Chol-*dit*', and I remembered her fears that she would never see me again. This wasn't real. I prayed, Please God, let it be untrue, please save her . . .

My mind whirring around like a mad thing, I thought of all the suffering she had been through, the times my father had shouted at her and beaten her. I pictured the time he beat her when we'd left his mother in the grass when the militia were attacking us.

At that moment the tears started pouring out of my eyes. The other boys read the letter and their reactions confirmed the truth of what I had read. I cried for three hours and then became very quiet, avoiding everyone else, not speaking to a soul. My cousin Thomas Wour tried his best to comfort me, saying, 'It's a war, everyone is dying.' I refused to believe she was dead, yet I believed she was dead, both at the same time. It was unbearable. In the end, I managed to put it in God's hands. I made a new resolution: if anyone came from my area, I would not ask for news. News was always bad! I had to surrender to fate. Whatever the future held for my mother, there was nothing I could do about it. I realise now that this denial of news was what you would call my 'defence mechanism', my way of leaving some doubt about her death, and some hope that she was alive. Something as conclusive as her death was too much for me to take so suddenly. So I talked myself into imagining how much unreliability there could be in the news I had heard.

After six months in Sudan, Kuot returned.

He brought a sombre but not unexpected picture of what was happening in Sudan.

The bombing over there was worse than when we had left. The SPLA were a constant menace, trying to recruit boys to fight. I felt vindicated, not going with him in the first place. Garang came back with him but Matouh never showed up. Kuot said Matouh had joined the SPLA, and I never heard of him again.

Besides that, I was relieved to have Kuot back with me. He and Wour were my closest friends, and they would get me through the worst time of my life as it slowly sank in that I had lost my mum.

But also at this time, there was an incident that would eventually cause us to leave Ogujebe.

There was a disco in the camp every Friday and Saturday night, where they would play Congolese music, which was rhythmic and instrumental and gave people some relief in the joy of dancing. There were no age restrictions, and sometimes I would go there to watch videos. It was here that I saw a TV for the first time. There had been a television at the camp in Itang, but it was so competitive there, with everyone trying to watch it, a small boy like me could not get anywhere near it. Now that I was able to watch videos in Ogujebe, I was amazed and instantly addicted. I would go as often as possible. I was mainly addicted to movies starring Arnold Schwarzenegger or Sylvester Stallone, or *Walker, Texas Ranger*. It is strange, looking back, to think that at a time when my friends and I were renouncing war and soldiering, we were fascinated by films about killing people. Most of all, we loved kung-fu movies. After they were finished, we would run around and call ourselves 'Jet Li' and 'Bruce Lee' and practise kung-fu manoeuvres. That was pure fun.

The disco and video area was between the dormitories, surrounded by a tightly knit grass fence. There were revolving coloured lights and when they had the music blaring it was an exciting place to be. They didn't serve alcohol, but lots of people got drunk in other places, then came to the disco and got into fights. Being too young to drink, I couldn't understand this kind of violence and kept as clear of it as I possibly could.

The disco was a particularly dangerous place to go if you were Dinka, as I discovered when Mour Mour was killed there.

I had first met Mour Mour in Nimule, where he was working for the SPLA's intelligence unit. It was his job to seek out and arrest people who were suspected of crime within the region. He seemed to like his job; it gave him a sense of worth to be contributing to what he saw as the administration of justice.

Mour Mour was very smart, well respected, and athletic. In his mid-twenties by then, he was light-hearted and loved to make others laugh. Despite his military background, he would never have hurt anyone. His downfall was his attachment to drinking.

He would go to the disco every week and on this particular night he got involved in one of the regular fights. He was with another Dinka man, Manute, a hard guy who had spent time in the Cuban army after being taken there from Ethiopia.

I never knew for sure, but I often wondered if someone at the club that night had been arrested by Mour Mour at some stage. Or it may have been random, who knows? But Mour Mour was set upon by a large group and kicked to death. Manute was also bashed, but managed to escape.

It spelt bad news for us Dinka if two of the oldest and toughest men in our tribal group could be attacked like this. After Mour Mour was killed, we all grew anxious and insecure: we were worried that we were next. Even though bombs were falling everywhere in Sudan, some of the boys chose to go back there rather than be the target of Acholi gangs in the Ugandan camps. I wasn't so intent on continuing my education there if going to watch a video meant risking death.

After the murder, Kuot, Wour, Atem, Arop, Samuel and I were among a group of Dinka taken to Par Kela, a small town with a UN store about three hours' walk away. The United Nations had decided it was safer to put Dinka into Par Kela than to try to separate us from the Acholi in the huge camp at Ogujebe. Many other Sudanese tribes often blamed the Dinka for starting the war, because John Garang was Dinka and he had founded the SPLA. To my mind, this showed that they did not understand the causes of the war. The Acholi had suffered greatly from the fighting, but being further in the south they had not been invaded as we had by the Muslim militias. All they could see was what was nearest to them, which was armed Dinka men fighting in SPLA uniforms. So they saw us, wrongly, as the aggressors.

The camp was one mile from the local town of Par Kela. It consisted of two big buildings, looking like old factory warehouses, surrounded by a lot of trees. All the boys lived together. People who were married or had families were in one building, single boys in the other. There was a shared kitchen where about six hundred people would get fed, and it was first in, first served. If you were late, you could wait for hours.

Par Kela housed members of the Ugandan army and United Nations staff. The houses of the town were mainly built along the side of the bitumen main road, and many of the families had businesses out the front of their houses. Mostly they would sell tomatoes, food, cigarettes, or other wares that they had brought from the bigger markets at the town of Adjumani. The Lord's Resistance Army had been looting Par Kela constantly, so even though the Ugandan army controlled it there was a feeling of depression and fear in the town that never seemed to lift.

The United Nations people were generous to us in the camp. Nevertheless, we felt isolated because we were not allowed to move around very much. The more we moved, the more we could be a target for other tribes who hated the Dinka.

A Sudanese church minister called Father Joseph Ayok used to come to the camp every morning and every afternoon. It was the first time I had seen a black person married to a white person – Father Joseph's wife Karen came from England. I had heard about England from looking at the maps in school at Pinyudo. He had adopted many aspects of white culture – he used to hold his wife's hand and was affectionate to her in public. We all expected her to behave like an African woman, but when she went to get water she would carry a jerry can in her hand instead of carrying it on her head. She was very friendly and popular. She was pretty, with long blonde hair and green eyes, and drew crowds everywhere she went. Boys would find any excuse to go up and talk to her. She charmed us all with her warm smile. But she was also a very strong woman. People asked a lot of her – to find them clothes, food and so on, and she would go out and get it done.

Father Joseph was tall and muscular. He and Karen were in their mid-thirties or perhaps early forties. He loved soccer and always wanted everyone to play. He would play as well, and sometimes Karen would referee. Joseph treated everyone the same and always with respect.

There were about a hundred of us there who had no family, among a thousand or so other people, most of whom came from Sudan. Father Joseph was one of our Dinka people, but missionaries had taken him to England as a young boy.

Before long we had to move again, because it was better to put us in a big dormitory at a proper school rather than the improvised situation in Par Kela. The hundred orphans, as we were called, were to be moved on to Adjumani. But the good news was that Father Joseph had bought some acres there, and we were allowed to live in tents on his land, about five to a tent in a group of twenty tents. We had to choose our groups, and here I would live together again with Kuot and his brother Garang. Garang was always arguing with people and no one ever wanted to share with him, but we decided to let him stay with us because Kuot and I knew that if he got out of hand, together we could overpower him.

It was Kuot's job to make sure that all the tents were clean and that the boys were looking after themselves. A lot of the boys needed guidance, and were lucky to have anyone at all who cared about them on a personal level. I worked with Kuot to help supervise the boys who would not clean themselves or do as they were told. I would either give them plots of land to dig or, if they chose, they could be beaten instead. Not many chose a beating, which was good, because I didn't like doing it.

Seven of the orphans were older than the rest of us, and we held them up as our elders and looked to them for guidance. We had members in charge of food and agriculture. At night we would take a cold shower by taking a jerry can into the bush behind the accommodation area and tipping it over ourselves. For breakfast we would have porridge. If you were on breakfast duty, you would wake up at 3 am to go and get the water, light the fire to heat the water, make the porridge and so on. The firewood was collected on a Saturday morning, a duty that was shared by everyone. Sometimes we would find maggots in the porridge, and we had no choice but to eat it. If we refused, we would just starve. After repeatedly finding maggots in our food, we devised a system of draining the porridge through a mesh.

It was in Adjumani that my education got going again, at the Biyaya private school. It was crazy, but there were no resources to split up the ages and teach us in different classes – there were students of twenty learning alongside kids as young as four. I questioned the humanity of the teachers sometimes too. They were rough. The Maths teacher, Mr Henry, was about twenty-four and was short and muscular. He did karate. He was from Uganda and belonged to the Madi tribe.

The Madi tribe were well known for showing their emotions publicly. When Madi gathered for a funeral, there was lots of drinking, lots of music and *lots* of crying. It was strange to me. In Dinka tribes, when someone dies we are just plain sad and don't want to do anything.

Along with these emotions, Mr Henry was violent. He used to thrash us with a cane, and the whole school was afraid of him. Older boys would want to fight him, and some even threatened to kill him, but he never seemed afraid. Most Madi people are friendly. They would rather talk through a problem than fight. But Mr Henry was different.

The headmaster didn't ever do anything to stop him, and he was rough as well. His name was Mr Burndoro, also from the Madi tribe. He was a better man than Mr Henry, though he never seemed to enjoy life. He walked around with a mournful expression on his face, and on the rare occasions when he laughed it was in a singular loud burst that seemed unnatural. I sometimes felt sorry for Mr Burndoro, because we used to give him a hard time. We would steal his lemons, and mix the juice with water and sugar. We loved it! He wasn't a bad headmaster really. At 10 pm every night he would come and do rollcall. He knew all hundred of us by name, he knew who was a troublemaker and who was not. One time, seven of us went into Adjumani camp to watch a video and on the way back Mr Burndoro met us on the track. It was about ten o'clock at night and he was riding his pushbike. We ran away from him instantly, recognising that we were in trouble. He raced back to the dormitory on his bicycle to do his rollcall. We made it back just before he did and managed to bluff our way through, saying that we had not left the camp. He was angry, but all he did was yell at us: 'Back, mental!' It still perplexes me to this day, even though my English is so much better. I have no idea what he meant. All I know is that he would yell it at us repeatedly when he was angry.

Unlike Mr Henry, Mr Burndoro was basically a good guy, and most of the students were keen to learn. We wanted to do well and play sport, and as a result we began improving the school's image. We were getting a reputation for being well rounded: we could debate, win soccer matches, and do our lessons well. Eventually we gave Mr Burndoro a Dinka name. We called him Deng Adok. Deng, for rain, and Adok, for gum. If you made a mistake he was going to stick to you like wet gum or glue!

We were given pens and books to write in, uniforms of grey shorts and a blue shirt with the school badge embroidered on the chest. We had no shoes and no underwear. What I learnt here was different to what I had learnt in Sudan and Ethiopia.

It was in Uganda, at the Biyaya school, that I first heard the name Australia. The teachers said it was a small continent.

I was confused, thinking that it must have lots of different countries like Africa. How could a whole continent have only one country? We saw a photograph of a kangaroo, which I found funny because it had a pouch – I had never seen an animal like it. We learnt about Aborigines: that they lived in the forests, that they were also Australian but that you couldn't go to where they lived. (Later, when I went to South Africa, I was taught that Australia was the most racist country in the whole world!)

Sometimes it seemed to me that since I had left my village violence had followed me around. Even Uganda, which I had looked forward to as a kind of paradise, was erupting in warfare, murder and death.

Northern Uganda, where I was, had been terrorised by the LRA for almost twenty years. A lot of killing had happened between Adjumani and the nearest big town, Gulu. Buses and trucks travelling between the towns were often ambushed and robbed, and everyone was nervous when travelling. Villages were burnt down every day, and there were constant killings. Due to a lack of government control in the north, there were no proper hospitals or health-care systems. People were dying from a host of different diseases – typhoid, cholera, sleeping sickness spread by tsetse fly, malaria, malnutrition, lack of medication. The average life span for a Ugandan woman was between forty and fifty, for a man even less. Many of the population were affected by HIV and AIDS even then, and those who escaped direct contact with the war were often hit by the virus. AIDS was one of the few things the country seemed to unite over – there was a community-wide terror at the epidemic.

For the two or three years I was in Uganda, I never saw pictures of the president, Youri Maseveni, and it was hard for the government in the capital, Kampala, to reach the people of the north with either aid or communications. And this, compared with Sudan and Ethiopia, was a relatively functional democracy.

Like a typical bully, the LRA targeted civilians and vulnerable people. By the time the government responded, the guerrillas had vanished again into the jungle and it was too late.

The hundred of us without families tried our best to work together. Often there was squabbling, but we also knew that the only way to survive was to cooperate.

One night two LRA guerrillas came to rob Father Joseph. They got past the security guard, broke into the house and threatened Joseph and Karen with a gun. They stole everything, taking what money there was and leaving Joseph and Karen fearing for their lives. Ugandan police came later that night and said they had arrested the two men in the town, but that didn't settle our fears. No one knew if it was an isolated robbery or part of a new campaign that we should be more concerned about. Eventually Joseph and Karen felt too threatened to stay and left to go back to England.

This was a terrible turn of events for us. Without Joseph's support, everything became hard again. Food rations shrank, and morale in the camp was ruined. Arguments broke out more frequently among us, once with devastating effect. Ring was a boy I had met back in Nimule. Early one morning, he was on cooking duty with a boy called Sebat. Ring was asking Sebat why he hadn't tidied up; they started to wrestle, and Ring punched Sebat in the chest. Sebat stopped breathing. Kuot was woken and gave Sebat mouth to mouth, then CPR (we had been taught basic first aid back in Nimule by Sister Shaun and Sister Rita). The first aid failed to work, however, and Sebat died.

Ring ran into the bush and was never seen or heard of again. We tried to follow him and eventually came across some footprints and a patch where he'd urinated and defecated, but we never found him. Ring was an athlete, a great soccer player, and he always encouraged us to play sports. He liked to mess around and laugh a lot. He didn't usually fight with anyone – this was the first time I'd heard of him being aggressive. In their argument, Sebat had said he was too sick to clean up. Ring hadn't seemed to realise that Sebat actually was sick. Ring always took everything as a joke, and this time he must have thought the joke was at his expense.

We heard later that Ring sneaked back to the camp to take his belongings. The police hadn't acted on Sebat's death, apart from doing a few initial interviews. They didn't investigate to the point of going through Ring's things. It didn't surprise us that they never found him. We heard that he had gone back to fight in the war in Sudan.

Kuot was the only one who'd got into the kitchen before Sebat died. The body was taken by ambulance to the mortuary, and Kuot was asked to sleep with it, maybe to protect it. He refused. No one was asked any further questions and it just seemed to disappear from the police's minds. There were no counsellors to talk to us, no Father Joseph, and we lived in despair. The impact of Sebat's death seemed more personal as we weren't supposed to be at war among ourselves. We were at peace within the group; his death didn't make any sense. We were all like brothers by now, we all had our own duties and talents that we spent time developing – soccer, athletics, high jump, long jump and so on – but we associated these activities with Ring, and after he left we lost the heart for games.

It took us a couple of months before we started to heal. Sebat's cousin was Malek and Ring's cousin was Deng. They were now the next generation of the two families, and we were worried that one would take revenge against the other. But Malek just ended up lonely. No one seemed to support him, and in fact the opposite was true: most people seemed to be against him. He remained angry at Sebat's death and refused to understand that it was an accident. Deng was younger than Malek, smaller and incapable of defending himself, and everyone was afraid of what Malek would do to him in his anger. They came from different regions, and some of the people in the camp thought that it may have been an underlying tribal issue that contributed to Malek not understanding. The camp was united in trying to get the two to see the event for what it had been.

We were also stressed because Ring and Sebat were well-known at school. By the time we went back to school two days later, it was all the talk. We had to talk to all the other kids about the whole thing – we relived it over and over with each explanation. Ring had been very popular at school, so the event sent a shock wave throughout the campus. Even the teachers seemed to be in a state of shock.

The whole thing affected me very deeply. I had first met Ring in 1992, and we went to school together, played together and worked together. I felt terrible that Sebat was dead. I felt terrible that we didn't know where Ring was. I didn't want to see Ring punished more than he should have been, but if he had stayed he could have proven that it was an accident. By fleeing he made it seem as though he'd done it on purpose. I was angry at him for running away, for killing Sebat in the first place, and finally because it was all so unresolved and we were now left to pick up the pieces.

Amid this feeling of loss and insecurity, we began to think that the LRA or the Ugandan government would come to our camp at any time and take us to fight in their armies. We had no security. Authority was represented only by the headmaster Mr Burndoro, but what would he be able to do? He had his own family to protect. With Father Joseph gone, we felt truly like orphans. The food was decreasing, we were constantly being punished at school, and there was no one to turn to. Joseph would have given us the shirt off his own back, but now we were lucky to get any clothes at all. Any hope we had was fading fast.

By this time, the LRA were frequently coming into the camp, shooting and looting. The SPLA were also coming in, taking young boys with them to fight back in Sudan. I hid from them, feeling confused about the situation. I didn't want to fight, but if I had no choice, then maybe it was best to go back with the SPLA because they at least would give me a gun to protect myself. Either way, stay or leave, my life was increasingly at risk.

Deep down, I believed that to go back to Sudan would be like committing suicide. I would go back for only one reason – to follow my dead brother. I had survived too long to die so easily. And I wouldn't have my mother to return to. That weighed heavily on my mind. I was now faced with a terrible decision: going back to Sudan was suicidal, while staying in Uganda somehow seemed even worse.

One of Father Joseph's relatives had told us of a camp in Kenya, from which boys were being taken to America. Of course, we all knew of Manute Bol, the Sudanese basketballer who had become a huge star in the American NBA. I had been in Nimule when Manute Bol had visited around 1992, but hadn't been able to get close to him with all the crowds and cameras. He had done more than anyone to build ties between southern Sudan and America.

At school in Adjumani, we had written to penfriends in Michigan, at a school called Olive Elementary. Father Joseph had given them our names, and they had written to us personally and sent their pictures. We wrote back about our lives, although sometimes this made me sad as my life had so little in common with those kids in Michigan. But this part of my education had brought America into the picture, and I shared the belief of

116

many young Africans: living in a white person's country would be like living in heaven. I decided to go to Kenya, driven by the idea of getting myself to America.

This was a huge turning point for me, as it was the first time I really contemplated giving up on my country, leaving what was left of my family behind me and starting a new life in a different part of the world. But it was an intoxicating idea. I could go to America and study and work – and, most of all, feel safe. Just the idea of it provided me with new hope and allowed me to think of new possibilities.

I told Kuot about my plan and asked him to come with me. He said we should first get into secondary school in Uganda, but I didn't think I would be able to do that. I wasn't even finished primary school! I thought that if I stayed, Uganda would finish me. I told him I didn't want to waste time. I wanted to move to the next country that would give me an opportunity to go overseas.

So I decided to leave Kuot and all my other friends behind. I walked out at night. I had some books and blankets, but left them all to Kuot. I kept some clothes and my school uniform. I walked an hour to a camp nearby called Mire, where the younger Dinka boys had been sent for their protection. I stayed for a week. The night I finally left, I went back to the school. I wanted to spend my last night there, to say goodbye properly to Kuot and my closest friends. Mr Burndoro had been looking for me all week, and still was. He was furious with me and would thrash me within an inch of my life. All the kids wanted to talk to me, but Kuot kept them quiet so I could hide from Mr Burndoro. No one had told the headmaster that I was back there, as it would have come back on Kuot. The headmaster wanted my uniform back but I wanted to keep it to remind me of the school, the friends that I had there, and Father Joseph.

My last night in Adjumani, Kuot and I didn't sleep at all. We stayed up all night talking about how Kuot would follow me.

We laughed a lot. Kuot was busy talking about how he wanted me to buy him books and clothes when I was rich. He wanted books on English grammar, maths and physics. He was a good student, and knew that he would continue through to high school. Usually the teachers were the only ones with the books, but Kuot wanted his own.

I was excited about moving on, but worried about the challenges I was going to face along the way. My first challenge was closer to home. As I went to leave, I spotted Mr Burndoro before he had a chance to notice me. I just ran.

Kuot caught up and took me to the bus stop.

After this, I would have to find my own way. Even though Kuot and I were laughing, we each knew how sad the other was. We had been close friends since Nimule, and I trusted him more than a member of my own family.

I had saved enough money, seven thousand Ugandan shillings, for my fare to Gulu, which was the next big town to the south and the transport hub for roads east to Kenya.

The bus, like most buses in Uganda, wasn't a scheduled service but a vehicle on its way to Gulu that would pick people up along the way. I joined about ten people sitting on top of the goods they were going to sell in the town: blankets, cartons of oil, maize and beans. It was a long ride, leaving around seven in the morning and arriving at four in the afternoon, even though the total distance was only about a hundred kilometres. Everyone travelled in fear, as hundreds of civilians had been killed on this road. The LRA had stopped a lot of buses, stolen the goods and harassed or killed the passengers. Sometimes as a result of these attacks, all transport on the road was closed, for as long as a month at a time. For a while, when it resumed, the Ugandan army would escort the buses.

We were all afraid, and soon no one was speaking. The road

was bumpy, meandering through thick forest, and the driver had to wind the bus along the narrow road to avoid the land-mines planted along the way. Some small towns that we drove through were deserted – not one single inhabitant remained. We began to pass a lot of Ugandan army posts, so we relaxed for a little while and felt safer. When army vehicles escorted us for small sections of the trip, we started talking again. Even in the safer areas, however, we passed a lot of houses that had been burned to the ground.

My first impression of Gulu was of a nice, civilised city. On the way in to town there was a colourful billboard welcoming visitors. We passed a high school: it was big, much bigger than my school in Adjumani. Its size and impressive façade excited my imagination: I wondered what it would be like to learn there.

In Gulu there were big open parks. At one of them, Pope John Paul II had come to pray with the locals. It was a place that I had wanted to see. I was dazzled by the city. There were so many cars, the most I had ever seen in one area. They were banked up in actual traffic, not just isolated cars passing every now and then. The shops were bigger than any I'd seen, and sold different kinds of groceries. We stopped on the roadside and I jumped off the bus and looked for a place to eat. There was a milk bar like nothing I'd ever seen before. It sold nothing but milk, both plain and flavoured. It had tables and chairs, and the tables were covered in white tablecloths. On the top of each table were small white bowls of sugar and carafes of water. I went in and sat down, feeling impressed but also intimidated and shy. I looked at the signs to see what type of food I could buy, but it seemed they only sold milk. I ordered some, and was brought a jug of sour milk to which I added sugar. It was one of the best things I'd ever had. I bought glass after glass, guzzling it down. It was the first time since my home in Panaruu that

I'd had a lot of milk to drink. I never thought I'd miss milk so much!

After four jugs, they told me they wouldn't sell me any more. They told me my stomach would burst. I was so full, I had to sit there for a while. I didn't need to eat that night. We got talking and I told the people at the shop that my father had more than 2000 cattle. They laughed at me, refusing to believe that a skinny young boy who had wandered in from the street could come from such a prosperous family.

I went to stay in the cheapest hotel I could find. It seemed clean and reasonable, and I was able to stay there for one week. But everything was costing me money, and mine was running out. Every morning I would go back to the milk bar. I met some other Sudanese there, who told me they were staying in a local garage for free. I ended up there for another week, during which one of the mechanics talked to me about the possibility of working as an assistant to one of the drivers. I wasn't interested because I saw how the others were treated. Some guys at the garage also talked about robbing banks, and one of the mechanics who had wanted me to work with him went to Adjumani to rob a bank with six others. The mechanic was killed by the security guards during the robbery.

I wanted to keep going towards Kenya, but did not have enough money. Also, at this point the war in Sudan was going even worse for the SPLA. They had been pushed right down to Nimule – our soldiers were nearly being pushed out of our own country. I had a sudden flare of conscience and regretted my decision to go to Kenya. I did an about-face. I jumped onto one of the many SPLA trucks that were plying the road between Gulu and Nimule, and rode with the army back up to the border.

It was a big change of heart for me to dare to rejoin the SPLA. But beneath my rush of patriotism was the most basic reason: I had run out of money and couldn't see myself making it to Kenya on what I had. I could only see myself getting money by going back to Sudan.

Considering how I felt about the SPLA, and having run away from them before, it didn't really make sense – but I can only see that in hindsight. At the time, I thought I might get a paid job in intelligence, or as a radio operator, for the SPLA. I just had to find some money.

It was at a border camp that I met General Oyei, an SPLA leader who later became chief-of-staff of the national army in southern Sudan. I told him that I wanted to rejoin the rebel army as a radio operator. As my English had been improved through schooling, I was seen as an asset. But the general, who was a very friendly and smart man, said, 'Don't join the army. Finish your schooling.' He offered me a huge amount of money – up to two hundred thousand Ugandan shillings – to go back to school in Uganda. He said that the southern Sudanese cause needed educated young men now, not more cannon fodder. He gave me tea and a good talking-to. He said I should go to Kampala, the Ugandan capital, or to Kenya. After two weeks back with the SPLA, I took another army truck south.

I wonder what might have happened to me if this meeting with General Oyei didn't take place. I might have died in fighting, I might have survived . . . but whatever would have happened, this was the moment when my life changed course permanently.

Kampala was another twelve hours to the south of Gulu. I had heard that it was an even bigger city than Gulu, and people always talked about how nice it was. From there I could travel eastwards, into Kenya. As well as hearing that Sudanese like myself were being resettled from Kenya into the USA, I had also been told that refugees could get school scholarships in Kenya, and I thought I would give it a try. Education was my single focus now. I believed that if I could finish my schooling to a high enough level, I could do anything I wanted with my life.

I went searching for someone to give me a lift to Kenya. It would be a gamble to cross the border without papers, but I had no future in Uganda and it was the only way I could think of to get out. I asked a lot of people for help. Many were willing until they found out I had no passport. Some were still willing but wanted to charge too much money.

Finally I was re-connected with a Kenyan called David Kamau, who I'd met at the garage in Gulu. The truck depot for Kenya-bound traffic was next to the SPLA office, and drivers would often ask Sudanese boys for help. And if we saw a Kenyan, we would stick close to him. David was in his mid-forties, a very skinny man who drove a long truck with a trailer. He was a talkative guy, and as we drove he told me he could tell I was nervous about crossing the border, but he would make sure I'd be okay. We left Gulu at around 7 am and got to Kampala around 7 pm; we slept the night in Kampala, and the next afternoon we drove east towards the Ugandan–Kenyan border.

David would drive me up to the border and then into Kenya if I made it across – but I had to make my own way across the border itself. He would drop me before the crossing and then pick me up on the other side. He couldn't risk going to prison for me, so I had to be careful I didn't get him into trouble. This would be the first time I would try to cross a strictly patrolled border. There would be immigration officers checking for passports.

We arrived at the border in the early evening and David told me where I could go to cross by foot. He pointed out where the police were and described to me the place where he would wait for me on the other side. There would be a long line of trucks parked, he said, in front of a street full of food stalls and hotels. I would find him there – if I made it.

There were two ways across. If you went by car, you would be stopped at the official border station, have your passport stamped and possibly be searched. But there was also a pedestrian footpath, where the controls were much looser. On the Ugandan side were two police guarding a big wire fence, with a gate only wide enough for one person. On the Kenyan side, about another fifty metres away, there was another fence, also guarded by police. David said I would have to cross on the pedestrian path and hope that I was not one of the people stopped.

I didn't carry a bag, because if you had a bag you were an instant target for checking. I had only the clothes on my back and was hoping they would assume I was one of the thousands of Kenyans and Ugandans who went to and fro each day doing their business in the towns on both sides. This was a heavily populated area and it was not feasible for the officials to check the papers of every single person doing their shopping or going to work.

As I walked, I was almost disjointed by fear. David had said, 'Walk freely, as if you know the area.' I tried my best, swinging my arms and strutting like a local. My heart was thumping in my chest as I waited for someone to call out: 'Eh! Where's your passport?' But I must have impersonated a local pretty well, because I was lucky at both gates. I was only stopped when I had already reached the Kenyan side. It wasn't an official who stopped me – it was a man who made money 'helping' people who were crossing illegally. This man offered to escort me to Nairobi for money but my lift was already arranged. I went to the line of trucks and found David's. He was sitting in his truck waiting for me with some cold Cokes and Fantas. This had really been my lucky day.

CHAPTER 5

Kenya

IT WAS SEPTEMBER 1995 when David and I arrived in Nairobi. I lived with my new friend for one week, but life was difficult. I was in a big city, and everywhere people were dependent on money, to buy their food and to live. The intensity of this dependence was still new to me. Where I came from, we had nothing and no use for money. Even in the camps I had lived in, money was a secondary concern: you could always get by with nothing. But now I was learning that life in a free country revolves around earning and spending money.

David asked me to move out because he had a large family to feed and couldn't afford to keep me when I had no money to contribute. What little spare money he did have, he gave to me. Then he explained where I had to go: the United Nations office in Nairobi.

The UN building was in an affluent suburb called Westland, where a lot of the non-government organisations were housed. I talked my way through security and presented myself to the reception desk. The first official I spoke to told me to go back to the camps in Uganda, which was my first country of asylum.

No chance! After all I'd been through to get here, I wasn't going back. I ran out of the office, and with nowhere to stay I became a street kid for the next two weeks. I started to beg for money from rich-looking people. I felt so bad, my pride was destroyed – what would people think of me? I was asking people for food and money! What have I become? I asked myself many times. As bad as it was, however, I chose to beg rather than steal. I would go to the big hotels where people had money and enough education to understand my situation. It was ironic that some of them understood my situation quite clearly, even though I still did not.

Begging outside the Hilton, I met an American man called Gordon Wagon. He was bald, about seventy years old, and was wearing a white T-shirt and shorts. He said he had worked in Sudan, so he was familiar with the political situation and the fate of boys like me. He was in Kenya as a consultant to an NGO. He gave me some money for that night and made an appointment for me to see him at his office in Nairobi the next day. When I arrived, he gave me three thousand Kenyan shillings, worth about fifty Australian dollars. He told me to go to the camp in the west of Kenya, near the border with Sudan, known as Kakuma.

I didn't want to go to Kakuma. I had heard of this place in the desert where more than 36,000 Sudanese refugees were held. Even if some of them were being resettled to America, what hope did I have? They weren't going to send all of us, and I would be at the very bottom of the list. I lied to Gordon, saying, 'Sure, I'll go to Kakuma,' but instead pursued information I had heard about another camp called Ifo. There was also a resettlement program from Ifo, sending people to America, Canada and Australia.

Ifo was in the north of Kenya, in the Garrisa district. A lot of the people in the area were of Somalian descent. Most had travelled there as a result of their own war, but by now there were new generations that were considered Kenyan Somalian. It was also mainly a Muslim region.

In October I caught a bus to Ifo. In front of the camp was the UN headquarters: one large brick building. To the side of it were rows of white tents. The whole site had a feeling of being temporary, not just because of the tents but because, compared with other camps I had been in, Ifo looked like a dumping ground not worthy of being cared for like with pride.

In Ifo the situation was very different from what I had expected. I hoped it would be easy to get to America, but I was wrong. I applied to the United Nations to register me for resettlement but straightaway they told me that I was not eligible. This register was for Somalian and Ethiopian refugees only, they said. But I *knew* other Sudanese refugees ahead of me were registered. They got their chance to go to America – I was stuck. I found out that just before my arrival, the UN had changed its policy and cut the resettlement program from Ifo for Sudanese. They had been overwhelmed by the numbers. I was crying with frustration, but it did me no good.

I walked into the camp itself, which was surrounded by a fence made of thorns. Inside the fence were four camps for Sudanese refugees. There were hundreds of mud huts, not covered by traditional roofs but by tarpaulins stamped with the United Nations logo. It was not a good way for the UN to advertise!

I didn't think I could stay in Ifo for long, as life quickly became more difficult than in the other camps I'd been in. As I was not on the register, I was not receiving food from the UN. I was hungry twenty-four hours a day.

During the day, the camp seemed deserted. Ifo was always hot – every day was around 40°C. Often people would put water on the roof of their hut in an attempt to keep themselves cool, but instead it turned the water hot. People would either stay in their shelters or go into the bush and sit listlessly. There were very few tall trees within the camp providing enough shade to sit under. Many of the people in the camp had planted trees outside their huts in the hope that one day they would provide them with shade, but the trees were withered and leafless.

Ifo was a hotbed of rumours. People were always running around with new and conflicting information. A lot of them were suffering, sitting with nothing to eat, so they would grab hold of any snippet of hope. The camp was not the worst place I had been, in the physical sense, but the mood was absolutely desperate because the people all felt like they were so close to getting out of Africa but had been blocked at the last step. Ifo was a strange mix of high excitement and the most terrible despair and frustration.

The camp looked and felt like a prison. If you were outside after the gates were locked, it was hard to get back in. From a distance you could be forgiven for thinking it was a cemetery, the mud houses lined up like tombstones. The ground was covered in sand and on a windy day it was like a whirlwind with the sand flying around inside the confines of the fence. You saw people disappearing in the wind and enveloped by sand.

No sooner had I arrived in Ifo than I was robbed of the few shillings I had left. Now I had nothing. There was only one way to survive: I had to find a job in the camp. I ended up gathering firewood in the forest and selling it for a pittance to other refugees in the camp. Somalis feared going into the forest because of the bandits who lurked there. I was afraid of the bandits too, and did meet a group of them once. As I stood there tensely, they asked me questions about what stuff the other Sudanese in the camp had – they wanted intelligence on whether we were worth robbing! They wanted me to help sneak them into the camp. I said as little as possible, saying I was very poor, which was why I had to collect firewood for money. Seeing how low I was on the food chain, they let me go. I was lucky, because sometimes even if they found a Sudanese who had nothing, they would force him to carry their things for them.

I arranged with families to bring them firewood once a week; in return they gave me chapatis, tea, beans, and a place to sleep for a night. I would make some more food by offering to stand in the food queues for families who could not cope with the long wait. They let me keep a small food 'commission' – maybe some dry beans, or salt, or oil. I would build shelters, dig toilets three metres deep in hard ground in the heat of summer, anything to get food.

I still had my school uniform from Biyaya private school. I was wearing it one day when I was trying to sell a bedsheet for some food. Nobody was interested in the sheet, but a man offered to buy my uniform for thirty Kenyan shillings. I loved the uniform, and it was one of the last things I had of any value. But I was so hungry, I had no choice. For about a dollar, I lost it. And with it I lost a symbol of my hope to return to school; I was beginning to lose hope in all those ideas I had had about getting educated.

In Ifo I worked alongside Phillip Akot, a Sudanese guy who had been with me at Biyaya. We Sudanese were always popping up in the same places. It wasn't just coincidence. We were hearing the same information from the same people, so Phillip had followed much the same trail as I had, eventually hearing from Sudanese in Nairobi that Ifo was the place to go.

Phillip Akot was a garrulous guy who loved to joke and make people laugh. He also loved to play soccer. In Ifo we worked together as a team and were like brothers. We shared everything: clothes, money, food. Then one day he suddenly became paralysed down his left side – it happened overnight and we didn't know what was wrong with him. It affected the way he walked and the work that he was able to do. At times he even needed help getting dressed. He was stressed beyond belief, not knowing what was wrong or if it would last. He went to the local hospital but didn't receive any treatment; his illness was a mystery. Eventually Phillip went back to Nairobi for medical attention, and he was cured. Once he was fit again, he knew better than to return to Ifo. The last I heard of him, he was travelling between Uganda and Kenya.

By January 1996, Ifo camp was falling apart. People were leaving because there was no aid coming in. There were looters living in the surrounding forest; at night they would come into the camp and demand money. If refused, they would turn violent. Three months into my stay they shot one of the Sudanese refugees in front of his wife and four children. He was an old man who tended a small shop selling tea and coffee. He was harmless and considered to be a leader within the community.

After his death the camp's security was increased. The fence of thorns was now built higher, and the gates to the camp were all closed by 4 pm. The people responsible for the shooting were never found. Instead of them going to prison, we were the ones whose fences grew, we were the ones being imprisoned. Not feeling protected by the authorities, people started to protect themselves by making spears and other home-made weapons.

Ifo had originally been designed to be a Somalian camp, but with the influx of Sudanese refugees it had been divided into tribes. In Sudan 1 there were 500 Anuak people; in Sudan 2 there were 4000 Nuer people; in Sudan 3 there were 7000 Dinka people; and in Sudan 4 there were 10,000 Equatoria people. Setting up the camp this way created a new reason for conflict, as food and resources were not evenly distributed amongst the groups. Sudan 4 were given the majority of the rations. They were the ones who had arrived first and they were also the ones who had the most money. This meant that they were able to buy ration cards. With a card they could get oil, maize and beans every fortnight. Without the card, people like me got nothing. The card was also reflective of your registration as a refugee – without it you basically didn't exist. The other camps had a limited supply of ration cards and were kind enough to share their rations, and I was able to get by through the generosity of other Dinka people there.

Sudan 4 also had the advantage of having the chairman of the Sudanese community among them. Because he and those close to him were being looked after, he didn't seem to care about the plight of those of us who were struggling. Those who had money were setting up businesses, selling the meat of animals they had caught in the forest. They would sell rabbits, bats and small gazelles. This would be boosted by sales of sugar sold by the teaspoonful, wrapped in paper. The profits from the sale of the sugar were huge: most of the people in the camp didn't have enough to buy large amounts of sugar but could manage just enough to buy a small quantity even if the price was triple what it was worth.

The ones selling the goods were those who already had ration cards anyway – those who were hungry just grew more so and the divide between the groups grew with their hunger.

Within the camp there was a protection officer called Alpond. He had been a refugee himself but had been settled in America, only to return to help those back in Africa. To the best of my knowledge he was originally from Burundi. He dressed in hip-hop gear and had both of his ears pierced; he was in his late thirties and had a habit of swearing like a rapper.

Alpond had helped a lot of Sudanese refugees over the past couple of years, but unfortunately for me his generosity had run out by the time I met him. He was tired of not being thanked for the help he had given. He had the power to hand out ration cards and could also move you to the top of the list for being resettled overseas. Most of those he had helped in the past, he had never heard from again.

Some of the people in the camp decided that the only way they were going to get any help from Alpond was to bribe him. They set about collecting money from all those who didn't have ration cards. Unfortunately we had very little money and when the bribe was presented to Alpond he rejected it and told them to redistribute the money back to those it had been collected from. He had seen real money overseas, and wasn't impressed by the small amount we could offer. After he had rejected the money everyone knew that their options were limited.

Two weeks after the failed bribe, Alpond arranged for trucks to take anyone who didn't have a ration card to the camp at Kakuma where at least they would be fed. It was a decision each of us had to make for ourselves – go back to a camp with less chance of being resettled but have the satisfaction of food in our bellies, or stay put and hope for a miracle. I decided to stay put.

Rumours started to go around the camp that Kenyan officials would use force to get us to go to Kakuma. Some people fled into the surrounding forests, others disappeared and were never heard of again. Others walked all night and day to the Garissa district, an eastern province of Kenya, where they could find agricultural work on banana, onion and tomato plantations. Some just hid all day in the forest, and others went for refuge in Somalian communities, seven hours' drive away. Still I decided to stay, and the rumours were wrong: the officials never came and I was left safely within the camp.

Meanwhile the trucks arrived for those who had elected to go to Kakuma. Thousands left, making it easier for those who stayed behind.

As usual, peace didn't last long. Fighting was breaking out all over the camp as people became restless at the lack of support from Alpond. People were beginning to write to the UN about him not being willing to help them. Before long he was moved from the camp. It was terrible that all his good work and his sincere hope to come back from America to help ended like this.

No sooner had he left than the violence escalated. The chairman of our community was moved from Sudan 4 to Sudan 3, creating confusion over who was now leading the camp. It had been thought that, with the majority of people having moved to Kakuma, most of the problems relating to food rations would be solved as Sudan 4 would now be willing to share what they had with the rest of us. One night, people from Sudan 2 went to Sudan 4 for what should have been an evening of sharing and entertainment. Sudan 4 had set up small shacks from which they sold alcohol. A group of men from Sudan 2 had decided to spend the night drinking at one of these shacks. But they had no intention of paying for their drinks and every intention of starting a fight over what they saw as the unfair distribution of rations.

The fight started in Sudan 4 at around 5 pm and quickly spread. Seven men from Sudan 2, having had their fair share to drink, started to bash their hosts. The hosts used sticks to beat them off and the seven men retreated to find reinforcements. By 8 pm they had gathered more than a hundred allies, all eager to fight the men of Sudan 4. Together they went back into Sudan 4 armed with the spears, stones and sticks people had been making for self-defence. But by now the men of Sudan 4 had also gathered weapons. Rather than take the fight out into neutral ground, the Sudan 4 men stayed within their camp in order to protect what was theirs.

Despite the hundred men from Sudan 2 it was Sudan 4 who managed to win the battle. By the end of the night one of the men from Sudan 2 had been beaten to death as a message to the others not to return.

In the weeks that followed, the tension in the camp was extreme. Whenever someone went to get water or food, they would go with a large group. Those in Sudan 4 were particularly nervous because they knew that revenge would be waiting for them.

Three weeks later their fears were realised. Around fifteen men from Sudan 2 banded together to decide how best to pay back the murder of their friend. They had been keeping an eye on one of the members of Sudan 4, the only man not to stick with a large group when going hunting. The group from Sudan 2 waited until late in the afternoon, then attacked and killed him.

Later that night, to make sure their message got through, they cut off his head, placed it in a plastic bag and threw it over the fence of Sudan 4. Everyone panicked. People were crying and screaming. He was a victim of revenge for a crime he had not committed, as he was not one of those who had been involved in the fight that had started the whole thing. He was just a refugee like the rest of us. He had travelled by foot to get to the camp; like me, he had not seen his parents in a long time. He had a card and should have been getting ready to be sent to America.

Everyone grew even more afraid. No one would walk anywhere alone. The Kenyan police were tired of the Sudanese refugees bringing their rivalries to the local area. They threatened to close the camp down in order to restore peace. In the end they moved Sudan 4 to a camp three hours away called Dagahaley, while the Sudan 2 people were moved to a camp three hours away in the opposite direction. This meant that if they wanted to continue fighting they would have to walk six hours.

Only Sudan 1 and 3 remained. The camp became quiet. There were no gatherings any more, no one talked to anyone outside their immediate group, and any sense of community now seemed gone forever.

Food was becoming more and more scarce as time went on. In order to survive we had to become creative in the ways we sought and caught food. After the two other camps had been cleared out, we started to notice that the camp was attracting a lot of birds. They looked like small white doves – more importantly, they looked like dinner! The birds seemed to grow larger in numbers every day, and with our other food sources drying up, it was now crucial that we not waste the opportunity to nourish ourselves on the meat that was flying above us.

Every morning we would go out and set traps to catch as many of the birds as possible. The traps were made from material similar to fishing line. The line would be pulled tight at both ends with the majority hidden beneath the sand. At different sections along the line we would tie loose knots like nooses. Around the knots we would scatter maize and place containers of water to attract the birds.

Each morning they would fly down, thousands at a time. As they scratched through the sand for the maize their legs would get caught in the knots and when they tried to fly away the knots would tighten, trapping them. Sometimes each noose could trap up to twenty birds at a time. When they were removed from the traps their necks were snapped and then they were placed in boiling water for a couple of minutes to make pulling out their feathers easier. Once the feathers were removed their heads were cut off. They were now ready to cook. Most of the time they were simply put into a hot pan, as there weren't enough rations to turn them into more interesting meals.

The birds in the camp didn't only come from the sky. There were also large birds like pelicans that would walk around the camp. These birds were like us – they were starving, and by now they were coming to us for help. Normally these birds would fly away as soon as we got too close, but because they were hungry they would come to us hoping to be fed. Little did they know that they would be feeding us – in the pan alongside their friends from the sky!

By this time I was around nineteen years old. I say 'around' because I didn't really know. I didn't have any facial hair and I still looked like a boy. One of the men in the camp, called Panchol, who was distantly related to some of my cousins, took me into his group and looked after me. Around the same time, a new UN protection officer came to the camp who seemed to feel sorry for the Sudanese who were left behind and tried his best to get us registered with the UN as quickly as possible. I was considered too young to register by myself, so they nominated Panchol to act as my foster father and we could be registered together.

Finally I received a ration card of my own. In 1996, one year after I had arrived in Kenya, the UN registered me as Chol Biem Ngor. I would now be able to access the resettlement program, and going to America seemed just around the corner. We were all asked to write our life story so we could be placed in order of need. At last, this was our chance to find a way out!

But once again I was to be disappointed. I was beginning to ask myself if I carried some kind of curse. As soon as I arrived anywhere, the good times seemed to have just finished. If I had gone from Gulu straight to Ifo, I would have arrived at a time when American resettlements were being handed out like candy. The minute I arrived, they dried up. Now that I was registered with the UN, I found out that the resettlement system was full of corruption. People were paying the local UN representatives, the Kenyans, for their applications to be processed quicker.

I wasn't above corruption myself – I paid one official from Kenya for a position as a scooper, which meant I was responsible for measuring out the rations. I would measure out equal amounts of oil, salt and beans. People would always beg for more than they were entitled to. It was important not to give in, as there were supervisors conducting spot checks on how much everyone was given. I tried not to take advantage of the system and was never game to steal the rations for myself, but every now and then a supervisor would tell me that I had done a good job and could take extra for myself. If they were going to give me extra, I was not about to say no!

But although I could pay enough to secure a job as a scooper, I had nowhere near enough money to bribe an official to have me resettled. I could see lots of people around me getting resettled ahead of where they should have been in the queue. It was obvious that they had paid money to get ahead of people like me. I soon realised resettlement wasn't just around the corner. Some people had got to the point I was at – registered, with a ration card and a job – and then waited year after year, and they were still there. I could not afford the bribe and it became clear to me that I was destined to spend longer in this hellish camp than I could stand.

I have to tell you, sometimes I wondered if I was the unluckiest person in all of Africa – which is saying something! But I did not succumb to self-pity, as tempting as it was. I always looked at setbacks as a challenge to fight my way through, not a sign from the gods that I had no hope. I looked forward, not backward. Maybe this was my survival instinct. If I'd spent too much time looking back and feeling sorry for myself, I might have given up on life itself.

I decided to move on and try my luck somewhere new. I settled on Nairobi because I had heard that I might be able to get some kind of scholarship there to go to school. The information was unreliable, as always, but I pinned a lot of hope on it, as always. Anyway, it had to be an improvement on languishing forever in Ifo. Before I left I made sure that someone else was able to benefit from the scooping work that I had done. I gave my position as a scooper to a friend of mine called Aboui. The position had cost me two hundred Kenyan shillings in the initial bribe and was paid three hundred shillings a month. Or so it was said – I had had the job for three weeks and was yet to be paid anything.

I made a deal with Aboui. In exchange for the position he would help me with transport to Nairobi. He would get the pay that I was owed for my three weeks, and I would have the chance to leave and find a better life. I would leave my card behind with Panchol. I would stay in contact with him, and if my name came up for resettlement, I would return.

It never came up, so I believe I made the right choice.

I left the camp around May 1997 on a bus to the Kenyan capital. The journey was difficult because I didn't have any proper documents. Travelling without papers never allows for comfortable movement.

Whenever we came to one of the numerous police checkpoints, I tensed up, thinking I was about to be arrested. The police did come on board a couple of times, but thanks to pure good luck and the fact that the other people on the bus had legitimate papers, I was not asked to identify myself.

When I arrived in Nairobi I had nowhere to go. My plans for school had been vague at best. I felt lost in another big city, and out of place. I knew of places where Sudanese were living in Nairobi, but the central bus station was confusing – the destinations were marked with numbers, not places. I slept that first night in a big public park where a lot of homeless people were living. I wasn't scared of the street kids who came in to raid, because I had nothing of value to steal. Probably most of them thought I was a street kid myself.

The next morning, I decided that a church was the best place to go. I searched Nairobi until, shivering with the early morning cold, I came across Reverend Marks from the Born Again Christian Church. The 'church' was a big white tent near the park where I had slept. I huddled with his congregation and prayed. After the service, I approached him and he asked me where I was from. Seeing how cold I was, he took off the very nice leather jacket he was wearing and put it on me. 'Keep it,' he said.

Reverend Marks was a medical doctor as well as a pastor, with very light skin. His mother was German and his father was Kenyan. For the next four months he gave me accommodation with the street kids the church rescued. The deal was that you were meant to be 'born again', and I prayed with them for a new life. I liked the idea of being born again, but I also liked the idea of being able to sleep and eat for free. After they had given me so much help, I volunteered to help hand out food to street kids from the soup kitchens the church set up around Nairobi.

Here I met an old friend, called Williams Agar, from my Ugandan days. We worked side by side, and he was going to classes in English. Reverend Marks asked if I wanted to be sponsored to go to the school too, but I said I wanted to go further south, to Zimbabwe. Reverend Marks looked at me closely and said: 'Tell me when you are ready, and I might be able to help you.'

By August, I was ready to move on. Despite the kindness of people like Reverend Marks, Kenya had not been a happy place for me. The low point came when one of the street kids William and I had helped stole all of our possessions, including my prized leather jacket.

I told Reverend Marks I was ready to go, and he gave me fifteen thousand Kenyan shillings. The Tanzanian border was only a couple of hours south of Nairobi, and I boarded a bus in the hope of getting to Arusha, the first big town on the Tanzanian side.

As with my entry into Kenya, I thought my best chance of getting across the border would be to get out of the bus and walk through the pedestrian gate.

But I had forgotten how much luck I had needed to cross a border that way. I have never been blessed by especially good fortune, and was probably unwise to believe that I was about to get lucky twice in a row.

CHAPTER 6

Tanzania

AFTER DISMOUNTING FROM THE BUS, I walked clean through the gate on the Kenyan side of the border . . . and then through the gate on the Tanzanian side! I felt confident in my acting skills now. I must have really been looking the part of a local.

But the Tanzanian side was swarming with police, army and immigration officials. Fearing that I was about to be tapped on the shoulder, I went into the immigration office and stood in the queue like a legitimate passport-holding traveller. I waited there a while until I was near the head of the queue and the police presence seemed to have thinned out, and then ducked quickly into the street as if I had had my passport stamped.

There was a guesthouse with a restaurant where new arrivals waited for the bus to Arusha, about sixty kilometres south. While I was sitting there having a cold drink, a man came up and said he could help smuggle me out of here. I pretended to take affront. 'What are you saying? I have a passport!' I said. He said: 'I know you don't have a passport. Give me money and I will help you get to Arusha.' I suspected he might have been a police agent, so I brushed him off.

A little later, as I was still sitting there, one of the chief immigration officials came in. I don't know if I had been informed on by the 'smuggler', or if the official just thought I looked illegal. He said: 'Show me your passport.' Of course, I had nothing to show. I spent my first night in Tanzania in a concrete police cell with a couple of others whose luck had also run out.

The next morning I was deported back over the border into Kenya and handed to the Kenyan police. They asked if I had money. When I said I did, they took me to a bus that was heading back to Nairobi and told me to pay for my fare while they were watching. If I didn't pay I would still have to go to Nairobi, only as a prisoner, and I would stay even longer than I wanted to. So, to get away from the police, I chose to pay.

I got on the bus and kept to myself for the first kilometre, then asked the driver to stop and let me off. I would not be shaken – I was going to Tanzania. Again, I would have to walk, but not through the gate this time. I would head south-east, towards the foot of Mount Kilimanjaro, where there were no roads and, I hoped, no patrols. It took me a day and a half of trekking up steep hills and through thick forest, using only the cloud-shrouded volcano as my guide. I knew that if I kept heading south I would eventually hit a road well south of the border.

While I walked, I passed Masai villagers who greeted me. I saw gazelles, snakes and other wildlife. I greeted the people politely but didn't stop until I came to rest under a tree. While I was there, some local boys came up and we started talking. I said to one in English: 'If I give you two hundred Kenyan shillings, will you go back towards the border and find a bus driver who will stop for me?' Most of the transport was small Kombi vans that sped straight through to Arusha. The boy looked dubious. I said: 'If you can do that, I will give you another eight hundred shillings when I get on the bus.' A thousand Kenyan shillings was probably more than these boys would see in a year.

The boy went, and I waited for a couple of hours before he returned with two men in an empty minibus. One was the driver, the other the conductor. They wanted ten thousand Kenyan shillings to travel a little more than one hour! I knew this was extortion – it cost fifteen hundred Kenyan shillings to go from Nairobi to the Tanzanian capital, Dar es Salaam, which was about a twenty-four-hour drive.

I refused, and they said: 'Okay, we are going.' Actually I wasn't just outraged by their demand, I was afraid of them. I felt that if they knew I had ten thousand shillings, they would bash and rob me.

For a few minutes I tried negotiating a lower price, but they knew they had all the power. Eventually I agreed to give them the ten thousand shillings, which left only four thousand in my pocket. It was a bad deal for me, but I had no choice. There was no point keeping my ten thousand shillings and being stuck in the middle of nowhere.

We got into the bus, and after twenty minutes we came to a police checkpoint. The men told me to hide under the seats. I heard the conductor talking, and the driver motioned me to stay down.

After another twenty minutes we arrived at a small town, where the men told me to get into another bus that would take me to Arusha. I said: 'But I have paid you to take me to Arusha!' They said they would pay for my ticket – which turned out to be no more than three hundred Kenyan shillings. Then they drove off as fast as they could.

I sat down on the bus next to a woman who was, to be polite, very large. She wore a long grey Western-style skirt with a loose red blouse. As we turned each corner I could feel myself squashed harder and harder between her and the side of the bus. My situation was worsened by the overwhelming smell of chickens, both live and dead (they smelt as though they had been rotting for days), and dogs that, although small and harmless, were vicious when it came to their odour.

The sun seemed bigger and hotter than ever, and I was covered in sweat. The human aroma on the bus told me I wasn't alone! Each time the bus stopped for a break everyone rushed out to urinate under the shade of the trees.

We were now on our way to Arusha, and I felt as though my journey had a new impetus. As much as I was pleased that I had made my next move, I also knew that my final destination was not Arusha. I was committed to a long journey with many more stops along the way.

Arusha was quite a large town but not well developed compared to the Kenyan cities I had seen. My first night's accommodation was paid for by the large lady I had met on the bus. I couldn't speak the native language, Swahili, and she couldn't speak Dinka, but together we managed a few words in English. It was enough for her to understand that I needed help finding a place to stay. She gave me enough money to eat and sleep for one night in a cheap but comfortable resthouse. I handed over the money at a desk and was given a key. The single room was bare, but warm enough and safe enough to rest my soul for the night and it was certainly better than I was used to.

The next morning I caught a bus to Dar es Salaam, the capital. There were no tall buildings I could see; compared to Nairobi, it was a confusing and scattered place. Once I arrived at the bus station, I began searching for my next place to stay. I found a hotel, but could only afford one night. The next morning, as usual, I focused on a church. I found another Catholic convent, where I spoke to the sisters and brothers, catching them early in the morning and joining them for their morning prayer. I thought that if I could show I was a good Christian, they would be more likely to help me. I was wrong. No sooner had I finished praying than they kicked me out, locking the gate behind me. So much for the power of prayer! I walked for the rest of the day around the town, trying to find somewhere to stay. I tried seeking out other Sudanese or foreigners in the hope that they would help me.

I was wandering outside a church when I came across some kids playing in the street. I went up to them and asked where I could find Sudanese people. One of them, a tall, well-built Tanzanian about my age, replied in English. He said he would help me find the Sudanese embassy. We introduced ourselves. His name was Douglass.

Douglass hailed a taxi, gave the driver some money and told me to get in. He assured me that we would find a place where I could get help and perhaps somewhere to live. We drove through the streets of the capital, which were narrow and dusty, with cars and bicycles flying in every direction. When we arrived at the embassy we went to reception. The staff asked in English what we wanted and instructed me to sit down. Douglass left, giving me his phone number on his way out. I spent half an hour waiting for someone to see me, and was given tea while I waited. Then I was called to the office by a short, muscular man who wore dark glasses – he looked like someone out of the *Men in Black* movies I'd seen in Ogujebe. When he sat down next to me I noticed he had a pistol strapped to his side. I became shaky. An instant ago I'd been thinking I was getting help, and now I was *needing* help – fast.

He asked me where I was from, what tribe I belonged to, what language I spoke. He shoved a map of Sudan in front of me and asked where I was born. Most of all he wanted to know how I came to be in Tanzania and if I was a member of the SPLA. My answers were vague and didn't seem to make him very happy. He asked me again why I had left Sudan. I told him that it was because of the war, and he told me there was no war. No war? I thought he was either from another planet or some kind of spy trying to trick me.

I was taken into a white room where they took my photograph. They told me they were going to make me a Sudanese passport. I was taken back to reception and given some money for food. They told me to go and buy some lunch, then to come straight back. This I took as my opportunity to run. The combination of the gun, the questions and the photographs made me nervous enough to risk giving up whatever help I may have received. I didn't think I was about to be made more legitimate. I thought I was about to be deported.

I ran to the nearest public telephone and rang Douglass. He told me to find a taxi and gave me directions to his house. When I got there, the evening was already dark and cold. He was living in a nice house with his parents. Douglass gave me a blanket, some hot tea and bread, and told me I could sleep outside. His mother didn't seem happy to have me, so I was even more grateful to Douglass for helping. I slept there for three nights.

Throughout my journey, some people have helped me and some have turned me away. Some have listened to me with open hearts, and others have suspected me as if I was a conman. Some people have been scared of me because I have such dark skin, and others see an honest man in desperate straits. I have wondered about the reasons why one person can be so different from the next, and I can only say that it comes down to their different experience of the world, the disposition of their heart, or even their mood on the day. In Douglass's case, he understood my English and simply felt sorry for me, and he felt so strongly that he was doing the right thing, he was prepared to defy his parents. He was a good man.

Realising that Douglass could not solve my problems, I again contacted the United Nations. It was a dead-end: they told me to go back to Kenya. If I stayed in Tanzania after my illegal entry and without a passport, they said, I would be in breach of the UN Convention. I had travelled to one country too many. If I was to be resettled in a country like America, it had to be from Kenya, the UN said. But there was no way I was going to return to Kenya, and they couldn't force me.

I stayed in Tanzania for ten days. On the ninth day, I went to the Church of Christ where they gave me money and told me the same thing I had heard at the UN – go back to Kenya. I was hemmed in. Kenya was not an option, and to stay in Tanzania would mean risking jail or, even worse, forced deportation back to Sudan where the government, realising I must have been with the SPLA, would either throw me into jail or even, I feared, kill me.

I couldn't go back, and I couldn't stay here. I could only keep going forward; and forward, now, was Malawi.

CHAPTER 7

Malawi

THE BUS TRIP TO MALAWI TOOK TWO DAYS. Having learnt from
my previous experience, I decided to take the bus only as far as
Kyela, the town before the border. The rest I would cover by
foot.

The bus had to stop in the town overnight, so I used the
vehicle as my accommodation, lying to the driver that I would
be continuing my journey the next day. I don't know whether
he believed me, as I certainly must have looked like an illegal,
but he consented.

During the night I went into the town to gather information
on how best to cross the border. I went to outdoor food stalls
and asked the sellers. They had nothing to gain from deceiv-
ing me, so I thought they would be the most reliable sources. I
asked what the border was like, how to cross it and what would
happen to me if I was arrested. Near the bus station a woman
in her forties, with a scarf covering her hair, wearing a pinafore
that she stuffed with the money she earned at her food stall,
offered to organise some people to help me across the border
but she wanted me to pay her. I agreed, and fifteen thousand

Tanzanian shillings changed hands. After that, I had about a hundred and twenty thousand Tanzanian shillings left (about 100 Australian dollars) – it sounds like a lot, but it wasn't, and I felt very vulnerable to being swindled because I had no idea what a fair exchange rate was into Malawian kwachas.

I returned to the bus to sleep, waking up constantly throughout the night, worrying about what would happen and how my crossing would be achieved. I was worried that if the police didn't get me, the local magicians would, or the traders that sold human body parts, all of which I'd heard about in this area. I was being overtaken by my fears, but for good reason, I felt.

At 4 am I left the bus and returned, as agreed, to the woman I had paid. We met at the plastic-covered stall where she worked. She was with two men in their early twenties who would take me across the border, but not in the way I had thought. They now told me there was a safer route that would take us twenty kilometres upstream of the town, along the Songwe River that divided Tanzania from Malawi and flowed into Lake Malawi. We would travel by bicycle. One of the men would ride one bike, while the second man and I would share the other. I didn't have any suspicions about the change in plan. They were open, friendly seeming people, and I had placed my fate in their hands.

The roads were winding and very bumpy. This trip was a pain in the butt – literally! We were told that the point where we would cross the river was shallow enough to wade across, but when we got there we found that it wasn't. The banks sloped down gradually, and a lot of cultivation took place on the edge: it looked tranquil enough. But the water was deep and the currents strong, especially for someone with my sketchy swimming ability. The men decided we would have to use one of the small wooden boats being hired out by ferrymen waiting on the riverbank. This trade was low-key and certainly illegal.

The boat was so small that only three people could cross at any one time, two of whom were the men running the boat. They needed to be paid (everyone needed to be paid), and they would take me on the first trip, coming back for two more trips to collect my escorts. I was suspicious. How was I to know that once I had crossed, the other two, whom I had already paid to take me all the way to the first main Malawian town of Karonga, would join me? I decided to take some security: I would carry one of their bikes with me. If they wanted their bike back, they had to follow me across. I figured the bike was worth more to them than not following.

I could tell they weren't happy; they spoke to each other in their own language, but I knew from their body language that something was going to happen. Eventually they agreed and gave me one of the bikes.

I got to the other side and waited anxiously for them to follow. The boat brought them across. I breathed a sigh of relief and the journey continued.

We were now on the Malawian side of the border but still had five kilometres before we reached Karonga, from which I could catch a bus to the capital, Lilongwe. My two escorts started to become aggressive. They wanted more money, whatever I had. I told them I had no more to give. They suddenly became angry, threatening to kill me and reminding me that we were now in the middle of nowhere. We were only five kilometres outside a small town but we may as well have been in the middle of a desert – they could do what they wanted. I was scared, and they knew it.

Again I told them I had no money, and one of them pulled out a knife. I was sure they were going to kill me. Backing away, I scrabbled behind myself and found a stick. I told them that if they attacked me, I would attack them right back – if they were going to kill me, I would not die alone. I only had the courage to do this because my back was to the wall. My experiences had taught me some cunning, too. They looked at me and saw a weak civilian, but I knew I was more powerful than that, I had army skills, and I wanted to give them the impression that I was a hardened ex-soldier. I might have looked aggressive and angry, but really I was scared. Yet this is no contradiction. I had learnt early in life, in Sudan, that the most aggressive and dangerous people are often the ones who are most terrified.

They gave a nervous laugh and told me that they had been joking. I told them that they would now have to lead the journey – the two of them in front on one bike, with me following behind on the other bike. I wasn't taking any chances. I was not going to trust them again.

We arrived at Karonga without further incident. Lilongwe was about five hundred kilometres away. I didn't know how far my money would take me. One third of the way along was the next main town, called Mzuzu. I kept my expectations low and tried to muster up the fare to get there. I had to exchange the one hundred and twenty thousand Tanzanian shillings I had into Malawian kwachas. My two escorts, on discovering how much money I really had, demanded that I allow them to do the exchange. I still didn't trust them but I had no choice. They let me know that if I didn't let them exchange the money, they would report me to the police.

They made the exchange and handed me back the money – or, at least, half the money. I told them I would check the rate and they assured me that they had not taken anything. But when I insisted that they come with me to check, they ran. I tried to chase them but couldn't keep up. In desperation I picked up a rock and threw it, aiming it at their heads. I missed – probably a good thing, for if I had got one of them I might have found myself in trouble for assault, not just for entering the country illegally.

By the time I arrived in Mzuzu it was about 5 pm. All the money I had was gone. I sat at the bus station wondering what to do. Would I now have to steal to survive? I knew I couldn't sink that low. I had been in this situation before, and it was not within me to steal. I started to think about telling my story to anyone who would listen, hoping they would give me money in exchange.

Not for the first or last time, my life story was becoming my meal ticket. It might be odd, for an Australian, to see your life story as your sole economic asset. But for me and other Sudanese who have little else to sell, it was the natural thing to do. I never had to create any fictional embellishment to my story, because telling the truth was persuasive enough! Even when people had their own problems, they felt pity and sorrow when they heard about mine.

People started giving me money, enough for me to invest in my stomach, but not to make my next journey, to Lilongwe. The people in Malawi were very poor and it wasn't likely that I was going to be able to get the financial help that I needed on the street. Again I returned to the church, this time a Catholic mission. I went there around 8 pm on that first night. Parishioners were filing out after Mass. I tested many people, by greeting them and seeing who would greet me in return. I raised my hand and smiled, waiting for a response. The person with the warmest response would be the person to help me.

I tried with many people, but not a single one returned my greeting. Then at last one of the priests looked at me with what seemed to be a kind face. He smiled and said: 'Hello, my son, how can I help you?'

I replied by giving him my life story, which by now was starting to feel long and convoluted. Between the father and a sister who was also drawn into my story, they decided I could stay in the mission. The sister thought it would be good if

I went to a seminary and became a priest. All I wanted was a bus fare to Lilongwe.

Eventually, after much negotiation over my soul and other matters, they gave me my fare of two hundred kwachas and drove me to the bus station. The sister then prayed for me. She asked for God to guide me along the way, she prayed for peace in Sudan and she prayed for peace around the world. I hoped for her prayers to be answered. As I left they told me of a Catholic church in Lilongwe where I could get help.

I arrived at Lilongwe at nine o'clock the next morning. As instructed, I went straight to the Catholic church, where the first person I saw was a watchman who tried to stop me from getting in. His presence, and his behaviour, made me worry. Why was there a guard at the church – and why would he stop me? I was a Christian. Was it because of the way I was dressed? (I had multiple layers of clothing, some getting pretty old, and I hadn't had a bath for three days, so maybe I just didn't smell good enough to go into a church.) The watchman told me to wait outside. I told him that I hadn't prayed for days – I was busting for a prayer!

Finally he let me in. It was a small church and there were only about twenty people at the Mass. I walked up the centre aisle and could sense that everyone was scared of me. I sat up the back and waited as the priest finished the morning prayer. Even though he was speaking to the whole congregation, he was looking straight at me; I felt as though everyone was staring at me. I could see what was going through their minds. I was different – my skin was darker than theirs – and at the very best I was a stranger, at worst a criminal.

At the end of the service I spoke to the priest. He wanted to know where I had come from and what I was doing there. Again I repeated my story, making much of the kind priest and nun I had met in Mzuzu. He gave me another two hundred kwachas and told me to go to the United Nations to find the nearest refugee camp.

I obeyed, trying my luck at the United Nations office in Lilongwe. They told me that they only saw people on Wednesdays. It being a Monday, I left, wondering where I would sleep for the night. I decided to go to the police, to see if I could get myself arrested and put in a cell overnight. I wasn't scared of being deported: this was too far away from Sudan; there were few direct relations between the countries, and this was an English-speaking, Christian country. Sure enough, they didn't deport me . . . but they wouldn't arrest me either! They kicked me out, telling me to go to the UN. Didn't they know it wasn't Wednesday? I contemplated doing something extreme to get myself arrested, but, remembering that I didn't have all the appropriate identification papers, I figured I could end up with a longer stay than I bargained for.

I went to the bus station to sleep, but it was unsafe. There were a lot of street kids, a lot of drunk people, and still everyone was looking at me as if I was an alien. To them, I was either a threat or an opportunity. I wouldn't survive the night, I could tell that straightaway.

It was now around 6 pm. I was walking along and I looked up: towering above me was a mosque. I had run out of ideas and options – I had tried everything. For no other reason would I ever consider going into a mosque.

This was the first time in my life I had gone into a mosque. Muslims had killed my ancestors, my grandmother, my brother, my friends and relatives, and they had destroyed my country. Muslims were our historical enemy. As Dinka children, we had always played games in which Muslims were the baddies. We had been taught to hate them from birth. Muslim aggression was the reason I was here, not at home.

But I didn't really think of these people as Muslims. I thought of them as Malawians – they were black, they were not like the militias from northern Sudan, and they looked identical to the Malawian Christians. To be honest, I wasn't thinking about the irony of seeking help from Muslims. I was thinking that they would ask me difficult questions about the Koran, or have me perform their rituals, and catch me as a fake. I was more worried about being found out than reflecting on the ironies of my situation.

Inside the mosque everyone was washing their feet, hands and face ready for prayer. I joined the queue and followed their lead with the washing. At least I hadn't been thrown out yet. We went into the mosque and lined up in rows. I went to the back row and stood by myself. The imam then led the prayers and everyone followed him. I didn't know all the words, I was just mumbling. The only words I knew, from Sudan, were 'Allah Akhbar' (God is great) and 'Mohammed rasul Allah' (Mohammed was sent by God). When these words were used, I lifted my voice and made myself heard. Throughout the rest of the prayers, I mumbled quietly, trying not to attract any unwanted attention.

Halfway through, I realised that I had in my pocket a New Testament Bible I'd been given by the Catholic priest in Mzuzu. I thought that if they found the Bible on me I would be burnt alive in the mosque.

The prayers ended and everyone went outside. Some of them gathered around me, and the questions started: who was I, where was I from? I gave them a Muslim version of my name – Ahmed Chol. They were all happy that I was speaking in broken Arabic, and thought my Arabic was good. They believed I was Muslim. I felt proud on the one hand that my masquerade was working, yet I also felt bad because I was betraying my own religion for the sake of getting help.

They asked me why I had left Sudan. I told them the Christians were killing Muslims like me. I told them that my family had fled and were now all living in Saudi Arabia. They offered to buy me a plane ticket to see my family there. I told them I didn't have a passport. I told them that an uncle was flying in from Saudi Arabia to meet me in Zimbabwe, and that he would help me with my passport.

These good, generous people offered to give me the money that I needed to travel to Harare the next morning. They asked how much money I wanted. I didn't want to say anything, in case they realised that my story was a lie. I told them instead that I just wanted a ticket. They promised it to me and then the prayers resumed. I grew tired – I was exhausted from this constant praying with my five-word vocabulary. I told them I wasn't feeling well and wanted to go to sleep. They gave me a place to sleep in the mosque compound.

The next morning, two Arab men with very long beards and wearing *djellaba*s drove up to the mosque in a dark green sports car – an Audi. The roof was up. They spoke with the sheikh and handed him some money. As I watched, something amazing happened: the roof of the car started to come down all by itself! Then it closed up again! I had no idea what was happening, and was afraid to ask. It wasn't until years later, when I was in South Africa, that someone solved the mystery for me. There were cars with roofs that went up and came down. Amazing!

Anyway, the money they gave the sheikh was my bus fare, and the next thing I knew I was in a bus travelling south-west to the border between Malawi and Mozambique.

The bus arrived at nightfall, so I had to sleep in the border town. A stop was good, because it gave me a chance to have a look around the border and plan how to get across it.

At nine the next morning, I arrived at the checkpoint. There were a lot of trucks carrying goods between South Africa and Malawi, but what I noticed most in my anxious state was the number of border patrol police. They were everywhere.

I was very nervous; I was sure I would be arrested at the border. Across the road from the checkpoint was a small restaurant. I was so hungry, I felt as though my stomach was trying to tell me that this would be my last day. I felt I was about to die unless I had food.

After warily crossing the road, I entered the restaurant. As soon as I stepped inside I noticed a Malawian immigration officer sitting eating his breakfast, steam rising off a fresh cup of tea. I nearly had a heart attack! I didn't know what to do. Should I run or should I stay calm? Sit and feed the hunger in my stomach, or scramble to some dark safe corner? If I had wings I would have flown away – if only I had wings. I was mumbling prayers to God in so many languages that even He must have been confused! My prayers became so frantic they combined into a tribal chant. I started to call on my African ancestors for help. Why did they not respond? Instead of the immigration officer vanishing into thin air, he finished his tea, looked straight at me and walked over. This was the end! He would ask for my passport, he would ask for my papers, he would ask many things. Please God, I prayed silently, open the ground and swallow me up now!

He was wearing a grey uniform and had a moustache and a large belly. He began to speak, asking questions but not those I had expected. He asked how I was, and where I was from. I was too wary to speak. I cautiously told him in English that I was from Sudan. He gave me his hand and said: 'Welcome to Malawi.'

I was confused and wary, but in spite of my suspicions I couldn't help being happy. He was helping me! Before I could say any more, I gave him my biggest smile.

'Thank you,' I said. 'You are a brother from another mother!'

He laughed. He told me he knew the suffering of my people and spoke of how he had followed Sudanese history. At that moment I was relieved beyond belief. Even if I was arrested now, someone was going to stand on my side.

But after this warm conversation, he said he had to leave to go back to his office. I watched him go, and made a terrible mistake. Not only had I forgotten to eat, I had forgotten to ask his name and take his details. I cursed myself. How I was going to contact him if I got into trouble? My good friend had just vanished. He didn't care that I was illegal – he just cared. And I had let him disappear into the crowd.

I decided to act as rapidly as possible – to get across the border into Mozambique. This seemed as though it was going to be the hardest part of my journey, harder than anything that I had done before. Maybe I was worn down by everything that had happened, but there was always a battle inside me between fear and hope, and at this point my fear was winning.

When it came to the border crossing, I was almost breaking down. I couldn't think straight, I was so afraid. I had to settle my mind and concentrate on doing one tiny thing after another. If all these things added up, I told myself, I would arrive at my destination. I needed a plan that was carefully thought out and broken into simple steps. I don't know if I was going insane or if what I was about to do was an act of genius, but either way my thought processes had slipped into fantasy.

I had noticed that the border was lined with trucks, one after the other in a never-ending line. To me, they meant a screen, protection from official eyes. I decided I was now going to be an actor in an action movie. I set my scene: I was a street kid on the run from the law. To escape I would crawl in slow motion, hiding behind the row of trucks to get to the other side of the border. My character had to have many layers to be believable.

I pretended to sniff glue as I went along, so that if I was caught they would think I was crazy. If they did catch me I would act like a crazy man, ranting and raving.

On my hands and knees I crawled, sniffing my empty drink bottle, giving the performance of a lifetime. I made my way beneath the parked trucks; I edged slowly towards the border. I was much more scared of the immigration officials than I was of trucks running over me. No one seemed to see me – was my performance going to waste? As I finally crossed, making it safely to the other side after crawling on a road behind a line of trucks on my knees, I decided I would give myself the award for best international border actor in a drama or documentary.

Chapter 8

Mozambique

I WAS IN MOZAMBIQUE for little more than twenty-four hours, but it was an eventful day in my life, to say the least.

There was no border fence between Malawi and Mozambique, but after my successful impersonation of a crazy glue-sniffer I still had to walk ten kilometres from the border to the first Mozambican town. It was the morning of a very hot day, and I was carrying my possessions in the usual way: I wore my three T-shirts one over the top of the other. Over them I had a nylon rain jacket, despite the heat. I wore tattered jeans and worn-out black school shoes from Kenya. In my pockets I carried my toothbrush, my pocket New Testament Bible, and a handful of Malawian kwachas. I still had no identification papers of any kind.

To my tired eyes, Mozambique looked like a poor but picturesque country. I walked between mountains, along the line of the trees bordering a stream. In the distance I could see farms cultivating fields of maize and people working outside their scattered thatch huts.

As cars were passing frequently, I decided to stick to the trees, about two hundred metres off the road. There were buses rumbling by, but I didn't want to hail one because I feared I would be caught and sent back. I knew there were Mozambican police somewhere about, and didn't want to fall into an ambush. I wanted to at least give myself the chance of running and hiding. As I walked, I didn't talk to anybody. If I saw a farmer, I would keep him at a distance and return his wave. I could not picture myself talking to them anyway, as I didn't know anything of the Mozambican language.

The last time I'd eaten was at the Malawian border – a cup of coffee and a couple of pieces of bread. I was thirsty now, as the sun rose in the sky, but didn't want to ask anyone for water. On the roadside they were selling mangoes and other fruit but I hadn't changed my kwachas so I couldn't buy anything.

I arrived at the town and sat under a big mango tree to survey the situation. On the road entering the town there was an immigration control station, so I got up and walked about six hundred metres to the right of the checkpoint, through a thickly populated village area. It was the rainy season and the ground was muddy and gluey underfoot. Then I hooked around the back of the border gate, walking cautiously, avoiding people, until I arrived at a bus stop.

It was early afternoon and I was very hungry. They were selling all sorts of goods, and I wanted to buy something to eat and drink, but I didn't want to talk for fear of being reported. Timidly I asked the stallholders for prices. Everything was one million. A cigarette was one million. I said, 'Huh?' It sounded like a lot of money. So many people were walking around with stacks of money. I became afraid, thinking this couldn't be real money. But I had to go to a currency changer. They were all milling about, offering the best price and fighting with each other. I changed three hundred kwacha (about fifty US dollars) for Mozambican money, and received a couple of million dollars. I was a multimillionaire! I could have made myself even richer, but didn't want to change more because I didn't trust the moneychanger I had chosen.

The first thing I wanted to buy was a jerry can of milk. There was a place with lots of jerry cans filled with white liquid lined up on the ground. I bought one and got onto a bus travelling on the one road inland into Mozambique. It was a decommissioned American school bus, such as they have everywhere in Africa, but it was no longer yellow; it was very colourful, like most African buses, with scenes painted on the outside that were meant to illustrate the countryside and the destination. The bus was full, and I squeezed into my seat and, feeling that I was mixing in with the crowd, I relaxed.

As I began to breathe easily again, I sat back and took a good taste of my milk – to find that it was African beer! It looked like milk, but it was the beer they make when they grind maize, let it cool, put in sorghum, ferment it, and leave it for a week. I was familiar with the stuff but it wasn't what I wanted now.

There was an old man sitting next to me. I didn't want to talk to him, but he insisted on chatting away. He called himself a doctor; he was a witch doctor. I was confused; he seemed friendly, but I was still too scared to interact with strangers.

The minute I tasted the beer, I offered it to him. I thought I'd get drunk, which I definitely didn't need.

He took it and drank gratefully. In English, he said: 'Where are you going?'

'South Africa,' I said. I was actually planning to go across Mozambique quickly and get to Zimbabwe, but I didn't quite know how and didn't want to ask him or to reveal my plans. I don't know why I said South Africa. It just seemed the thing to say. To change the subject, I asked him where he was going.

'Botswana,' he said.

I asked how securely patrolled the border was between Mozambique and South Africa.

'It is very secure,' he said. I had heard this too. The South African borders were the toughest in Africa. I would be sure to get arrested there. But the old man said the border between Mozambique and Zimbabwe was much easier.

I think he worked out my story without my telling him. He knew I was adrift and needed help. Before the bus trip was over, we agreed to travel together. I needed someone to communicate for me. What did he need from me? I didn't know yet.

Our bus was heading to the town of Tete, in northern Mozambique. We didn't reach Tete that night. We arrived in a town called Mozauze, about an hour short of Tete, at four o'clock in the afternoon. The old witch doctor said: 'We should stop and rest here.'

I disagreed. 'Why do we need to stop here?'

He wanted to do some business in this town. He was saying he could cure illnesses, he could help women giving birth, he could bring back love if you'd quarrelled with your wife, and he could help you improve your luck in business. I didn't have too many options, because I needed a guide, so eventually I agreed to stop there.

We went to an old hotel and walked up to the reception desk. My companion booked two rooms for us, but wanted me to pay for everything. I'd agreed to pay for the bus all the way to Zimbabwe, but I wanted to go quickly, not stop here and waste time. But I also wanted to sleep, so we stayed.

We went to our rooms. The paint was peeling off the walls, and people had scratched their names on the walls and the furniture. There was no sewage system—you had to go downstairs for the toilet, and flush it by pouring in a bucket of water. The showers were two floors down, on the first floor, but the taps were outside. So you had to fill a bucket, carry it inside and pour it over yourself, and that was the shower!

I was tired and wanted to rest, but soon the doctor came to my room. He wanted to sit and drink alcohol. Then he said: 'What can we eat?'

'Go talk to the cooks,' I said.

He went downstairs, then came back. 'We can eat chicken here, it's really good.'

I lay down on my bed and waited. Having to stop in this town with this man, and paying my money for two rooms in a hotel, was putting me in a bad mood. When the food came, I didn't want to eat it like that – it was just barbecued chicken and maize pap together, dry, on the plate. I wanted food the way I was used to, in a soup. I didn't want to just pick up a piece of chicken and eat it. It had cost a couple of million, a lot of money.

'Where is the soup?' I said.

The doctor told me to 'bite the chicken and eat it mixed with the pap'. We started to argue – about the chicken, about the whole thing. He said he didn't care for me or my complaints, and left me alone.

Early the next morning, around six o'clock, we went to the bus station. I bought our tickets to Tete. On the way there we came to one of the longest bridges I have ever seen, a suspension bridge called the Zambezi Bridge.

It was another hot morning and, as we approached the bridge, people were saying the police were stopping vehicles. This was the last thing I needed, but sure enough, we stopped and two policemen got on. They hassled the driver and inspected all the passengers closely. As a policeman came to me, I stared down at the floor. I was sweating heavily and my pulse thumped in my head. I would be arrested now, and taken who knows where. The policeman hovered over me, then called out to his companion and jumped off the bus, waving the driver on. I could breathe again.

We arrived in Tete, and as I looked around I could not help noticing how different the people were. Through intermarriage with the Portuguese, the Mozambicans had light skin and long hair. I kept staring; I had never seen people like this before. They were dressed in a more daring, Western style than I had seen before – the girls in miniskirts and the boys with baseball caps turned backwards. They stood in a relaxed, showy manner, with their shoulders slouched, making gestures that didn't look African to me.

I told the old doctor I wanted to get the next bus to Zimbabwe – no more mucking around. From Tete you could go either south to Maputo and then cross to South Africa, or go south-west towards Harare. I wanted to go to Harare because it was the shorter way and an easier border.

But the doctor said he wanted to stay in Tete for a while and 'do more business'. He'd seen I had money and wanted to waste my time and have me pay for him. He wanted to book another hotel, and he thought that after his success in the previous town I was in his power. We had an argument in the bus station that lasted through the morning. I was so frustrated. It was only a four-hour drive to the border of Zimbabwe. I couldn't bear to wait any longer! If I stayed in Tete, I would be inviting more trouble. At any moment the police might come and spot me and put me in prison.

Finally he said, 'If you want to go, go.'

I walked around saying to people in broken English: 'Zimbabwe – car – go?'

It was all the language I had. I spent a couple of hours doing this. Either they couldn't understand me, or they didn't want to help such a suspicious-looking guy. Finally a man told me that there was a place I could stand to get a lift to Zimbabwe. I gave him some money to buy a Coke, and he pointed out where to stand – there was no actual bus station, just places where people would congregate. I listened to people speak and when I heard some of them talking about Zimbabwe I attached myself to them, trying to look as if I was part of their group.

We waited there for a while, until a pick-up truck arrived and everyone started moving towards it. I said to the driver: 'Zimbabwe?'

He nodded. I gave him some money and jumped into the tray of the pick-up with the other passengers. There were five of us sitting on each edge – I took a corner, a little precariously – while a couple of elderly people and children were sitting in the middle, by our feet.

The driver wanted one of the girls to sit in the front with him. But then he said she would have to pay more for the 'special seat'. The girl said no. The driver kept insisting, but the girl refused. He ended up leaving her there. Their little quarrel might have saved her life.

We drove off. The driver had a woman and a man in the front with him. They had a jerry can and I thought I could see them drinking together. The driving was soon a little erratic. We'd seen signs saying *Landmines*, still left over from Mozambique's war of independence, so we didn't want the driver swerving off the road. I grew anxious about landmines. One of the other passengers in the tray wanted to change places with me, so I moved to sit near the cab, holding onto the bar. This day was full of small decisions that had great consequences later.

We were about thirty minutes from the border when I heard a noise. It sounded as though a wheel had come off. The car started weaving violently, then it went off the highway into the scrub. It hurtled out of control, bumping over the ground through the low trees and bushes. I couldn't see anything – I had my eyes closed, I was hunched down behind the cab, terrified. Despite all the things that had happened to me, I had never experienced such sudden and intense fear as I felt at that moment.

I thought a landmine must have blown up. But later I figured out that the driver had been drinking and speeding, and the pick-up had hit a pothole which exploded a tyre.

We smashed into a big tree and stopped. The engine hissed and ticked. When I opened my eyes there was no one in the tray. I didn't know what had happened.

I sat there, breathing hard. I'd hurt my ribs and stomach. The driver got out of the cab. He was crying wildly, and fell to the ground. I jumped out and sat for a while, then walked back towards the road.

People had been hit by trees or had been thrown out of the car. There were bodies everywhere, covered with blood. Some had bad cuts, and some were obviously dead. Some of the children and the old people were lying dead in the dirt. The driver got up and looked for his assistant. His assistant, when he found him, had been decapitated by a tree. The driver just sat there and cried with his head in his hands.

It was the first time I'd been in or even seen a car accident. I was in shock. Some children were crying, crying, crying. I was saying to myself, 'Oh my God, Oh my God.' I thought I was going to die with them in the middle of nowhere in Mozambique.

I made my way back to the highway to look for help. Another of the survivors, a young Mozambican man, came with me. Trucks were coming. I waved at them to stop. They sped past. Finally a South African bus stopped and the driver opened his window to talk to us. It was a modern bus with computerised doors, and well-off people sitting in the plush seats.

The Mozambican guy and I stammered: 'There was an accident, an accident!' We pointed over into the scrub where we knew there were children crying and badly injured people lying amongst the bodies. The driver and another man got out and looked, then walked back to the bus. They did nothing. 'We can't do anything,' they said. 'We'll tell the police at the border, and they'll come back and bring an ambulance.'

Then the bus drove off.

I was sitting by the side of the highway with the Mozambican boy. We tried to flag down another vehicle, and finally a big truck stopped for us. We showed the driver – he walked with us into the bush. Other survivors were either crying or lying around, holding their wounds. The driver couldn't do anything, but he brought some water. I asked if he could take me to the border. I was afraid of the police coming and asking where I was from. I did want to help the injured people, but I was in a terrible situation. Helping them could create a huge problem for me.

The driver said, 'No problem, get in with me.'

I sat with him in his cab. He had his bed behind his seat. He offered me something to drink. I kept asking about the Zimbabwean border, and the South African border. He said he'd take me into Zimbabwe if I could make my way across the border by myself.

'If you can get across, I will meet you on the other side,' he said. I asked if he could smuggle me over the border.

He shook his head. 'No, there are guards who will check everywhere, and if they find you, I am in trouble.'

More than ever I felt like a fugitive. I had done nothing wrong other than having no official papers, but having no papers led me to make other decisions that I wish I didn't have to make – like leaving the scene of a terrible accident. Yet I felt I had no choice. Stopping there in Mozambique would have been the same as giving myself up to the police and asking them to throw me in jail and send me back to Sudan. I had to keep going forward.

The border was an open, dry place, with houses scattered about. There was no big government building, just a checkpoint with people standing around drinking and eating and a few policemen not doing very much. I thought it looked easy to cross. They did not seem to be paying attention to who was coming or going.

The driver dropped me at a small hotel on the border where he said I could get help crossing. I went into the restaurant on the ground floor. I didn't want to rush into trusting someone to smuggle me across the border, and I had other priorities: I was very hungry and I needed to exchange my money.

On the menu was a picture of plates of rice with different meats and vegetables, with prices in dollars. I was getting confused about the money I had in my pocket. I didn't know if these prices on the menu were Zimbabwe dollars or US dollars. I asked the worker in the hotel if they accepted Malawian kwachas for a plate of food, and he said, 'Yes, you can exchange it here. What do you want?'

I changed my remaining fortune of twelve hundred kwacha for four hundred Zimbabwe dollars, which at the time were much more powerful than they are now. I thought he wasn't giving me enough, but I wasn't going to argue. I didn't want to create a problem.

I ordered a plate of chicken – properly cooked in a stew with rice this time! – and a bottle of Coke. Once I had eaten I felt better, and the hotel guy and I became friendly. He said, 'Sit in a corner, don't go anywhere.' He didn't want anybody talking to me.

After a while, I told him about the accident. I said there were people in a critical condition. He said he would tell the police, and left me.

I sat and waited, trusting him not to bring police back with him. Soon he came back and said a report had been made to the police but nobody, not even an ambulance, had gone out there yet. I thought about those children and the injured survivors who were in a terrible situation out in the bush. But I was scared to talk too much about it. I wondered how I could make the police more urgent without attracting attention to myself, but I couldn't see a way.

I kept asking myself why I didn't get hurt in the accident. A part of me thought the witch doctor was controlling my fate, and he had caused the accident because we had quarrelled. I told the hotel guy about my misgivings, and he said that maybe it was true, those witch doctors were powerful men.

The hotel guy was reassuring me, though, and being as helpful as he could. He kept saying I was 'the best man'. He made me eat until my stomach felt like it would blow up. I found out later that he should have given me six hundred Zimbabwe dollars, instead of four hundred. No wonder he was happy with me! But I didn't find out the correct exchange rate until I got to Harare.

He did help me across the border though, and if I'd been arrested the police would have taken all my money anyway, so I guess the 'bargain' was worthwhile.

He outlined the plan for me. 'You have to wait until 10 pm. I'm going out to get someone who will help you.'

A little time later he returned with a Zimbabwean man. He was about my height and age, wearing black leather shoes, jeans and a white T-shirt. He looked flashy, like an African-American, with very red eyes. He was extremely friendly, which should have put me on my toes, but appearances are often deceptive, one way or the other. He said, 'You want to go to Zimbabwe?'

'How much do you want?' I said.

He gave my clothes a long look. 'Just give me that jacket.'

Taking it off, I said, 'Have my jacket, that's simple!'

He said he'd take it later on.

He said he'd show me a safe way around the border. About a kilometre away, he explained, was a place where people had cut the fence. I wanted him to take me over. He said he couldn't, because he'd committed a crime in Zimbabwe and couldn't go back.

'So where do I go when I'm on the other side?' I asked.

He said: 'You will find a main road that continues from here through a Zimbabwean town. Walk straight along the road to the bus station and ask for buses going to Harare.'

It was now ten o'clock at night, and he said the bus driver would let me sleep inside if I paid for my ticket upfront. 'The buses leave at four o'clock in the morning when the police are still snoring,' he said, 'so you will be safe.'

The last thing I did was give the man my rain jacket. He was leaving me here, as he didn't want to get caught bringing me across the border.

I left Mozambique with my three T-shirts, my jeans, my shoes, my Bible, my toothbrush, a few hundred Zimbabwean dollars, and some haunting memories of the day.

CHAPTER 9

Zimbabwe

FOLLOWING THE ZIMBABWEAN MAN'S INSTRUCTIONS to the letter, I left the hotel, walked for ten or fifteen minutes through the outskirts of the town, and found the hole in the fence where he had said it would be. I went through the hole and kept walking. It was dark by then, almost midnight, but there were still people about on the Zimbabwean side. When they greeted me, I wouldn't reply. They could speak English and I couldn't. I felt that by opening my mouth I would be giving myself away.

I found the Harare bus, as directed, and spoke to the driver.

'I want to go to Harare,' I said.

'When?'

'Tomorrow.'

'You want to pay now?'

'Yeah!' I said, relieved and excited. The plan was working out! 'Can I sleep in the bus?' I asked.

'Yes, yes, get in the back.'

I climbed in. I had a full stomach, I didn't need anything to drink, and I had made it into Zimbabwe without being arrested. I was happy.

For a while I looked out of the bus window for police Land Rovers patrolling around. Compared with police in all the other countries I had been in, the Zimbabweans looked well dressed and organised. I'd have to be careful of them. I kept spying on them through the window. After a while I said to the driver, 'Can I go and pee?'

'Just go through the window,' he said. 'If you go off looking for a toilet you might find problems.'

Eventually I went to sleep. By four in the morning people were coming in from the villages with their vegetables to go to Harare market, three hours away. I woke up as the farm people were getting in. The driver gave me some water to clean my face, which I did hanging out of the window.

The moment the bus started to move off, I relaxed. I was relieved, big-time. I felt as though an oppressive weight had been lifted from me; maybe I could get through this challenge, and make it to a better life in this country which had given me so much hope. Along the way, the bus kept stopping for passengers to get out and buy and sell vegetables. With two Zimbabwean dollars I bought a Coke. The highest notes they had were a fifty and a hundred. They also had fives and tens. I could work it out. No more of these millions – they scared me. It is a sign of how badly things have gone in Zimbabwe in the last ten years that their money is now as worthless as the Mozambican currency.

We drove for about three hours and arrived in Harare at a place called Mbare, a thirty-minute walk from the centre of the city. It was a bright, busy morning. Mbare was an overcrowded ghetto, with people everywhere, cooking alongside the road, living and working in little improvised shanties. Buses were stopping to take people to all parts of Harare. Markets were selling cheap food – tomatoes, meat and fish. It was very noisy, with people arguing and shouting at each other. I decided to walk to Harare. I didn't want to wait around this place any longer than necessary.

174

As I walked, I could see the skyscrapers. Harare was easily the cleanest, most modern city I had been in. If I had gone straight from my village in Panaruu to a city like this, I might have fainted with shock. Now, though, after my years in other countries and my time in big cities like Nairobi, I was better prepared. Still, Harare was impressive.

When I got to the city centre, I wanted to go to the United Nations office. At first I was afraid, because there were security guards everywhere. When I saw them I hid, not knowing the difference between security guards and police, thinking that any man or woman in a uniform was likely to lock me up. Eventually I asked a man where the UN office was, and walked until I came to Harare central police station. I started walking very fast. Some policemen outside greeted me, and I greeted them back, not wishing to appear suspicious. They asked me where I was going and I had no choice but to tell them. Besides, I was lost. To my surprise, they told me where the UN office was without asking me for papers. All of a sudden I had a surge of confidence. Simply not being arrested felt like a huge step forward.

When I got to the UN office, they handed me a form to fill in and gave me cups of tea. It was now two o'clock in the afternoon and there were other people there who'd waited outside all night, but the kind UN officers, seeing that I was in a desperate situation, let me jump the queue.

After I had filled in my form, some officers came out and said they would take me to a transit place for new migrants. They were helpful people at the UN in Harare, compared with some of my past experiences with that organisation.

While I was sitting there, a Sudanese man popped into the office from nowhere and greeted me. It was Albino Garang, a young guy I'd last seen in Ifo!

I was ready to jump up and laugh and cry and hug him, but Garang motioned me to sit still and be quiet. If they knew we were friends, they'd throw us both out. But a lady at the desk had seen my reaction. She asked if we knew each other. Garang said: 'We're just greeting each other because we're both Sudanese, we Sudanese are always like this.'

Garang and I went outside and got something to eat. He had arrived here from Kenya the same way as I had – sneaking across borders, always heading south in the hope of something better. But although we had much to talk about and a lot in common, he told me that recognising Sudanese friends might get us all into trouble, because it would look like we were banding together to bring other Sudanese into Zimbabwe.

Garang said: 'When you go to the transit camp, there will be other Sudanese, but pretend you don't recognise them. It's a sure way to all of us being rejected.'

I went back into the UN office and sat quiet as a mouse until they called me in. I was happy and excited to go to the transit camp finally. I was thinking, I've made it, I'm in Zimbabwe!

At the centre of the transit camp was a big circular building with a very high wall around it. There was a school in there, and a hospital with a doctor. On the other side of the building was some land on which the residents could grow tomatoes. There were also pens with poultry, which the residents could farm.

There were other Sudanese who had been in the camp for months. They came and looked at me curiously. I knew some of them from Uganda and Kenya, but pretended not to. They were trying to talk to me, but I acted coolly. From the UN staff I received four blankets and a cooking pot, with oil, sugar, tea leaves, dried whitebait and five kilos of maize. Everything was given to me at the one time, enough food to last fifteen days until the next handout. And I received my accommodation: a brand new one-man tent. And soap! I started laughing. I'd been to so many places and never been given a fraction of this.

The camp was divided into blocks by the different nationalities: there were Congolese, Rwandan and Liberians as well as Sudanese. Soon my fellow Sudanese were helping me put up my tent. They brought electricity cables from the central barracks room for our area and connected up my tent with electric light! They also gave me a small electric stove and a green T-shirt with a hood. It felt like the height of luxury.

Soon I was chatting with the Sudanese boys, feeling right at home. They said that the next morning there would be English classes. It sounded good to me. That first night I lay down in my tent, safe and comfortable, and thought about all the problems and challenges I had faced. I felt as if I had reached the summit of a great mountain and had the luxury to look down behind me at the troubles I had overcome. It had been a long, long time since I had felt this satisfied.

I stayed at that camp for about six months. We could choose to go to school or do some business. I chose school. I was granted a temporary permit into Zimbabwe which I had to have renewed every three months at an office in Harare. The purpose of the transit camp was to assess us and work out what to do with us next.

After I had been there for six months, I was taken in for a long interview with a frightening panel of officials: a UN protection officer, the transit camp manager, a welfare officer, two guys from the Central Intelligence Organisation and another person from state security. Their main purpose was to find out why I'd come to Zimbabwe and to decide whether or not to give me more permanent residency papers.

They peppered me with questions:

'Why did you come to Zimbabwe?'

'Why didn't you stay in Kenya or Tanzania?'

'Why did you leave Sudan?'

I told them the truth: I left home because of war, I left Kenya because life was not good, I left Tanzania because I didn't feel safe.

'Now you are here,' they asked, 'what if there is war here, where will you go?'

'I will not go anywhere,' I said, trying to demonstrate my loyalty to Zimbabwe. It felt like a big trap and I had to pick my way through the questions as if they were landmines.

'If Zimbabwe is in trouble,' I said, 'I will stay here to protect Zimbabwe. Zimbabwe is my home.'

My interviewers burst out laughing. I was just telling them what they wanted to hear. They were used to this, but they'd never heard anyone play the game so enthusiastically!

Some weeks later I received a permit stamped STATUS GRANTED AS AN ALIEN.

My new status had a catch, however: I had to leave the transit camp. They came and removed my tent and camping equipment, including my blankets. These I wouldn't miss. During my time in the camp, I would wake in the mornings with my whole head covered in fibres from the blankets. These fibres were soon to be found all through my clothes. If you looked after them properly, the blankets lasted thirty days. If not, they'd last seven days. Our nickname for the blankets was 'seven days'.

Once I was outside the camp, the government gave me nine hundred Zimbabwe dollars a month. This immediately turned out to be inadequate. Renting a room in a house would cost six or seven hundred a month, and I could not simply walk out onto the streets and find a job.

Instead, I did what many others did: I slipped back in and camped with friends, unauthorised. Some other Sudanese and I would jump the fence each night. Security would come and check all the houses and tents. They knew who should be there and who should not. If they found us, they kicked us out – or we'd escape before they caught us. But we had nowhere to go outside, so eventually we made friends with a security guard and gave him food so he'd let us sleep in the camp undisturbed. Unfortunately he was soon replaced, and the new security guard was not as cooperative, so we gave up.

I started renting a house with a couple of Sudanese guys in a suburb of Harare called Arcadia. We weren't cut off from life in the transit camp – we just weren't allowed to sleep there. An organisation called the International Catholic Migration Commission (ICMC) sponsored me to go to high school, once I had handed over my nine hundred dollars for the first month. The camp then let me farm poultry as well. I helped look after thousands and thousands of chickens, and would sell the eggs. When the chickens became big, we killed them, processed them and sold them as meat. Then, with the profits, we could pay the ICMC back.

During the days we'd hang around the camp, going to English classes, doing activities in the compound like playing basketball or cultivating cabbage, onions and tomatoes. The different nationalities formed into groups and fought each other. There were always problems between the different nationalities. The disputes were petty: people would all want to cook at the same time, but there were only so many stoves and so there would be fights; people would throw your food off the stove if they found it there. In the end I knew I would be better off outside the camp, but it was hard to break loose because it was so difficult to exist on the nine hundred dollars a month.

Because I came from a country without a proper education system, and I'd only learnt bit by bit in different camps in different countries, I was behind with my lessons. I felt it keenly. By now I was about twenty years old, and my reading and maths standard was no better than a twelve year old's. I couldn't seem to understand simple English, which was extremely frustrating. It just wouldn't go into my brain.

With the other Sudanese in the house, we pooled our money for rent and food. The sponsorship didn't provide for books or uniforms, so we had to buy our own textbooks and exercise books and decent school shoes. As a result, sometimes we had to go to school with an empty stomach. All I could think about in class was how hungry I was. In the end, if I didn't have any money for food, I wouldn't go to school.

There was an SPLM office in Harare, in the same building as the African National Congress, who were now governing South Africa. When we had problems, this was where the Zimbabweans would send us. Sometimes I would go to the office on the weekend with the other Sudanese boys and sit with the officials to talk about our difficulties. They financed their operation with a bar that was very popular with wealthy Zimbabwean and foreign men. We would see politicians and dignitaries from all around Africa visit the bar, buying a lot of alcohol and giving the SPLM some money in the process.

Now that I had residency in Zimbabwe, I was no longer scared that the SPLM would kidnap me to recruit me into their cause back in Sudan. But this didn't mean the SPLM was helpful. The head of the SPLM office was called Dr Benjamin. We'd tell Dr Benjamin about everything we needed and how frustrated we were, how we needed help to afford housing and education, and how we couldn't contact our families. By now, my people in the south of Sudan were suffering starvation – the next phase of the government's assault. Unable to win the war, the Arab militias were destroying the crops and livestock. Things at home were worse than they had ever been.

Dr Benjamin did provide us with some help. Through him, I got a message about my father. He had been shot in the leg during the fighting, and his friend and bodyguard had been shot dead. I couldn't speak to my father myself: like all the messages that came through, it was second- or third-hand.

Sometimes Dr Benjamin helped by giving us shoes, but he could only patch things over temporarily. Ours were the kinds of problems that never ended.

Obviously, though, I was happy to hear my father was alive after so long without any news of him. Hearing your father has been shot isn't always good news, but it was for me! Still, I felt distanced from him. I was a different person now, compared with when my mother had died. I wasn't so close to home, and my final destination, by now, was somewhere different from Sudan. I didn't know where, but I knew it wasn't back at home. Nonetheless, I thanked God that my father had only been super-ficially wounded.

Soon after I heard about my father's injury, our frustration boiled over. We were sick of the SPLM clearly doing very nicely in Zimbabwe, without passing on any assistance to us. So with two of my friends – Benjamin Bol Bol and James Makur – I went into the bar and smashed all the glass bottles. Dr Benjamin had collected beer bottles from around the world, and in our rage we smashed them all. Dr Benjamin, who carried a gun at all times, came in and screamed that there was 'A coup! A coup!'.

The police came and arrested us, and we were put into a prison cell. We were hassled by other prisoners until we told them we were inside for murder. Then they left us alone, and we had a comfortable space around us to sleep.

Because Dr Benjamin was saying we were staging a 'coup' – he said, incredibly, that we had been sent by the Sudanese Embassy to disrupt the SPLM – some officers of the Zimbabwean Central Intelligence Organisation came to interview us. They wore dark glasses and were very cool, but we knew them. They'd been regulars at the bar! Soon it was obvious that we were just frustrated young men, not political operatives, and the last body we would ever work for was the Sudanese government. We convinced the CIO agents and the police that we were just angry at the lack of help we got from Dr Benjamin. They even took our side. When we refused to eat the prison food, and the police feared we might starve ourselves to death, they badgered Dr Benjamin to send us better food. After a week we were released without charge.

For the first time, Australia came into my plans. I'd heard about a distant cousin of mine called Mayoum Mijok who moved to Australia in 1998. His mother's father and my father's father were brothers. That made us cousins, or uncle and nephew – sometimes these relationships are too complicated to untangle! All I knew about Australia was the little I'd been taught in Uganda. But it didn't matter that I only knew a tiny bit about Aborigines and kangaroos. A country like Australia offered me untold dreams.

I called Mayoum and asked him to send me a form for resettlement. I filled it out and took it to the Australian Embassy, who told me that I needed a recommendation from the United Nations. I took it to the UNHCR office, and they said they would get back to me. I never heard from them again. Despite my efforts to locate it, they couldn't find my form or any record of me. I suspect my case was thrown into the too-hard basket.

While I was in Zimbabwe, I was able to make a phone call to England, to Father Joseph who had looked after us in Uganda. I asked him if he could sponsor me to go to a Zimbabwean school. He sent me forty English pounds, and said I'd need to gather some education paperwork. But as I was doing so, I lost his phone number and was never able to contact him again. It made me very sad, almost as if he had died. My friendships with many people on my journey were like this – I knew so little about them, often all I had was one scrap of paper with a phone number on it, a tiny thread connecting me to another country. When that scrap was lost, the thread was broken.

By 1999, when I was twenty-two or twenty-three and had been in the country for about two years, the Zimbabwean economy began to deteriorate. Suddenly everything was expensive, prices jumping four or five times in one day. Violence spread in the streets, and sometimes we were attacked at night. It just started happening – people were being robbed everywhere, it seemed that either there were no police or there was no longer any respect for the law. There was suddenly a lot of hatred in the air. As 'aliens', we felt we were going to be a target for this violence. After all, that had been our experience before. When there is unrest in a country, people turn on the most recent arrivals, as if they are somehow responsible.

Most of the Sudanese boys had to decide now whether to go back home or not. I didn't want to return to Sudan because I felt I hadn't achieved anything. I couldn't speak English, I had no money. If I went home now, my situation would be the same as when I'd left, probably worse. My mother, my sister, my grandmother were all gone. I hadn't spoken to my father in years. Southern Sudan was a mess. I felt I had nothing to go back to.

Others among us wanted to go further, to South Africa, but we knew how hard it was to cross that border without being arrested. With the documents we had, there was no chance South Africa would let us in. But things were quickly becoming very bad in Zimbabwe, and we could see that it wasn't safe for us to stay.

***

I had a Dinka friend in Zimbabwe called Daniel Jok. His mother was white and his father was a famous Dinka called Dr Francis Deng, who had worked for the UN helping internally displaced persons throughout Africa. Back in 1978, Dr Deng had interviewed my great-uncle Makuei Bilkuei, who respected him very much.

Daniel was the second of Deng's four sons. He'd studied in America and was now working in Zimbabwe for a relief organisation. He was living in a nice big house with security cameras – when he invited me there, it was the first time I'd seen this kind of thing. He had a swimming pool and he was very excited when he saw me and my Sudanese housemates in the camera.

I had heard that Daniel had been giving Sudanese boys money to go to Kenya and South Africa. Some were living in his house. When we sat down, we told him about our concerns. We laid out our entire histories for him. Daniel felt the sadness of our stories in his heart, knowing that his father was from Sudan. Then, very tentatively, I told him things were so bad in Zimbabwe that I wanted to move to South Africa.

'Sure,' Daniel said, nodding. 'Call me tomorrow and I will see what I can do.'

When I spoke to him the next day, Daniel said he would give me five hundred Zimbabwe dollars for my journey. I had to travel south to Beitbridge to cross the Limpopo River. My journey had always been taking me south. South, south, south. It seemed like destiny, but I had a new idea now: I might get across the border into South Africa, hide there, and stow away on a ship to America, Australia or Britain. I had told this to some other Sudanese, who warned me that if I stowed away in a Chinese or Korean ship and they found me in the middle of the ocean, they'd throw me overboard.

I didn't tell Daniel this. He just wanted to help me get to the border – he wasn't involved in people-smuggling. He said the border was electrified anyway, and the Limpopo had crocodiles in it. You could only cross into South Africa via the Limpopo Bridge, but the immigration officials were well organised and they would arrest you. I felt that Daniel was giving me some assistance as a kindness, but he didn't think I had much chance.

And to be honest, going to South Africa wasn't the best option for me. But the idea of leaving Zimbabwe to the north and going back through all those countries I'd been through was exhausting and dangerous. I had come too far to turn around.

CHAPTER 10

South Africa

I LEFT IN A BUS LOADED WITH ZIMBABWEANS at two or three in the afternoon. I was the only Sudanese on the bus, which arrived at the border at Beitbridge at midnight.

Everybody jumped out of the bus, and my immediate problem was that if I stayed here overnight I wouldn't have a place to sleep. There were no hotels in this town.

There were men in the bus station changing money, and I went around asking them where I could sleep. I went to a bar at the station and grabbed a bottle of beer. As the night drew on, I became scared of being attacked. Everyone in the small bar looked threatening. I went back out into the bus station and asked a moneychanger how I could cross the border. I had experience with this now! He said he'd help me, but I had to pay him.

'No problem,' I said, 'I just want to cross.' I agreed to give him two hundred rand.

He talked to the bus driver who had brought me, and fixed up a place for me to sleep on the bus. He told me he'd come back at 4 am.

I slept until the man came with a hired Toyota Cressida and picked me up. He drove for two hours west of Beitbridge, not on roads but on bumpy ground. We arrived at a remote village with houses of thatched walls and corrugated-iron roofs. I didn't have a bag or anything; all that I had, I was wearing.

The guy stopped at a house, went in, brought me out a cup of tea, then went back in to talk to the owner. They came out: an old man and two young men about my age.

It was dawn by now. My friend was going back, but he said these people would take me across the border to the South African town of Messina. I started to become nervous.

'Am I in safe hands?' I asked him.

He said: 'They are going to take you inside South Africa. *Inside!*'

That made me feel warm in my stomach. They weren't just going to take me to the border and leave me to fend for myself.

Before leaving, the three men had something to eat in their hut and gave me a Coke bottle with water in it. We set off by foot, walking through the bush, hiding whenever we heard someone. We walked for about six hours until we stopped at the Limpopo River, on the Zimbabwean side. I still believed the stories I'd been told: if you put so much as your foot in the Limpopo, a crocodile would jump up and eat you.

Crocodiles weren't the only threat. There were helicopters patrolling overhead and we could see police motorcycles moving on the other side. There was a fence on that side, which the men said stretched all the way to Botswana.

The men knew when the helicopters and motorcycles patrolled. When they did, at a signal we lay down and waited until they had passed.

At one o'clock in the afternoon, my escorts said the border guards would be having lunch. Too desperate to give in to my fears, I swam and waded across the river at its narrowest point.

It only took about ten minutes to get across: myself, the old man and the two boys.

Now that we were on the South African side of the river but not yet at the fence, we had to lie down and crawl along the ground, like snakes. We crept along to a particular place in the fence, only ten metres from the riverbank. There was a patch of ground there covered with loose grass and sticks. The men had dug a hole underneath the fence. This was their secret!

They told me to crawl through the tunnel they had dug and walk for about twenty minutes until I came to a main road. But I said: 'The agreement was that you take me inside, all the way to Messina.'

One of the boys said he would go with me if I gave him the clothes I was wearing. I said no. I had very little money left, and I'd already paid two hundred rand to get across the border – the promise had been *Inside*!

But they were good at this. This was their business. They were thinking of robbing me. I could see it in their eyes.

I had an idea. I said: 'Do the police search people?'

'Why?' the old man asked.

'Because I have a gun.'

The old man said: 'Huh?'

'Yeah,' I said in my toughest voice.

They didn't talk about taking money or my clothes after that. They ran back to the river and swam across.

But although I'd escaped being robbed or worse, I was on my own now. So much for *Inside*!

After crawling through, the tunnel was short and deep under the fence. I walked to the main road as they had directed me. Modern cars were speeding past, making a great noise and wind. I was confused now: I didn't know what direction the town was. I walked westwards along the road, but it went a long way and there was no town. So I turned around and walked north-east.

Every time a car came, I hid in the bushes off the side of the road.

There were farmers cultivating cabbages and farm workers around, but I avoided them. I kept walking and grew very tired. I walked for hours, sweating in the afternoon heat, still not finding any town. I reached the stage where I was too tired to hide from cars.

Finally I came to a sign that said: *Messina 10km*.

I kept going. Only ten kilometres! That gave me great hope. But my mind was addled by heat, hunger, stress and fatigue. I saw a car coming, an army car. It went past me, about one hundred metres, then stopped and reversed. Was it reversing back to get me? I ran and hid next to a big tree and threw my identification, my hard-won Zimbabwean national ID, into the bushes. My status card might let me walk free in Zimbabwe, but it would get me deported here.

Sure enough, the army car came back. Sitting inside were some white soldiers. They jumped out and said in English, 'Eh, where you going?'

I told them I was going to Messina.

They said, 'Jump in.' They seemed good-natured. There were about seven of them in the car, holding guns. I wasn't going to argue.

We drove along the main road, but instead of continuing to Messina they took a turn-off before the town. My stomach was flying around with nerves. We arrived at a big military base, and they said, 'Come out, come out.'

I got out and sat down, waiting for the interrogation. I couldn't say I was South African. They'd ask me where I came from and I wouldn't know anything about South Africa. So I thought it would be better to say I was from Sudan than Zimbabwe. Sending me back to Sudan would pose a much greater problem for them. Maybe they would give up and let me stay.

There were more than a thousand soldiers in this barracks. One of the men who'd been in the car asked me how long since I'd eaten.

I just wanted them to leave me alone. 'Two days,' I said.

'Huh? Two days?'

'Yes.'

Another soldier came over. 'How long did it take you to come across from the Zimbabwe side?'

There was no point lying about where I'd just come from, but I could make the most of my story, and they seemed sympathetic. 'Two days,' I said, 'and I've been sleeping in the forest.'

They brought me some good food and drink. I tried to eat, but I was so scared I couldn't. I didn't know where they were going to send me.

One of the soldiers, a sergeant, asked me how long it had been since I'd left Sudan. I told him how I'd walked and caught buses from country to country for years. The soldiers who were listening were amazed. Some of them felt sorry for me, others less so. I said I'd been a child soldier, and they asked me if I knew how to use their guns. I said I even knew how to drive a tank. Soon I had them laughing.

The captain came and said they'd take me to Messina for the night, and then the next day a car would come and take me to Johannesburg. I was very happy – they wanted to help me!

They put me into a car and the next thing we were arriving at a police station in Messina. The soldiers said, 'Jump out here, and you can sleep at the police station.'

I didn't believe them. I sensed a trap and refused to get out.

They said: 'There's no problem, tomorrow the police will put you on a bus to Johannesburg.'

I got out of the army car. The minute the soldiers left, a policeman came up and said: 'Remove your shoelaces!' He shoved me and repeated the order. I was confused, and stumbled about.

They searched me, fingerprinted me and pushed me around very roughly. They wrote a report saying I had illegally crossed the border from Zimbabwe. They took my belt out, and my pants started to fall down.

A policeman grabbed me by the waistband of my jeans and threw me in a cell where there were about twenty men lying down. Seven of them were from the Congo. There was a Malawian guy, and a Kenyan, and two Mozambicans. I started to feel a little bit better, because I was the furthest from home and would be the hardest to deport.

A policeman brought us a slice of bread and a little bit of meat, throwing the plates wildly into the cell. I looked at the walls, which had been written on. One line said Williams Awang from Sudan had been arrested here on such and such a day. Another said Bol Bol, from southern Sudan, was arrested and held here. I wondered if he was my old friend Bol. I found a space and drew a small map of Africa showing where I was from. I went and lay in a corner, in my clothes, without a blanket, on the concrete floor and tried to sleep.

I woke up to a great clamour. They had arrested another hundred Zimbabweans crossing the border and were throwing them all in with us. The police knew them well: the day they let them go, they'd be arresting them again the next night. It was a big routine.

I was in the prison for eighteen days. There was one room with an open toilet, no door between the toilet and the other prisoners. If you wanted to go, you had to do it in front of everyone. Outside this room was a small courtyard where we'd sit during the day. The sun and rain would come down through the bars.

I was afraid here, because the police were so powerful and I was just a defenceless detainee on my own. Being ex-SPLA, I wondered if I might be able to claim political asylum. The big danger was that they would just throw me into prison for five years and forget about me. I had no way of knowing what they would do.

The prison was so overcrowded that I only had room to sleep huddled on the ground. Soon there was fighting. The food was distributed according to what country you were from, and the Zimbabweans got nothing, so they would sit there watching us eating our bread and drinking our tea. The guards wanted to give the Zimbabweans maximum disincentive to try to cross again, so they would punish them by not letting them eat a thing for two days. One Zimbabwean man was given no food for three days. He sat there, an old man, about to cry with anger, and watched me eating some meat. I asked some of the Congolese if we could all contribute a little bit of meat for this old man. They all said no. A Malawian guy said okay, and we pitched in together. I felt so sorry for that old man. The Congolese got angry, saying, 'If you want to give your food away, give it to us!' When I gave the old man the food, he was shaking and sweating. Next morning he was taken out and released, and he thanked us for sharing our food.

We joked about the meat, which was quite tender but strange-tasting. We'd say, 'They are cooking donkeys!'

I had my money hidden in a little slit I'd cut in the tongue of my left shoe. The police kept asking me, 'Where is your money?' I only had about a hundred rand (twenty-five Australian dollars), but I guarded it as if it was a king's ransom.

Eighteen days passed, and nothing happened. Then a man from the South African Department of Home Affairs came and said we'd be taken to court in the town of Louis Trichardt, about a hundred kilometres away.

We were put into a van and driven there, not knowing anything about what was going to happen, but hoping that in some miraculous way it might end with our release.

We arrived late in the day at a big prison building. Inside, everyone was locked into their cells. There were TV monitors showing the corridors and cells. The officers wrote down our names. While they were talking, I watched the surveillance monitors. In every cell there were things happening: people walking around naked and raving like maniacs. This was not like the Messina prison I'd just come from, this was a hardcore prison with inmates who had been in jail for ten, twenty or thirty years! I thought I was a dead man. I was just a skinny young boy. They would eat me for breakfast. My stomach started fluttering like crazy and I wanted to start crying.

Seeing our reactions, an officer said: 'No, we won't mix you with those guys; they've killed people and raped children and committed robberies. You'll be taken to cells for minor crimes and people on remand.'

I still didn't know whether to believe him. I was shaking with nerves as we were taken to a cell and pushed inside. There were about twenty of us from different parts of Africa, including a woman and her baby son from Congo. He was only about three months old.

We showered and were given food. We stayed in this jail for another seven days. On the eighth day they drove us to the court, but we couldn't see the magistrate yet. We just waited, waited, waited, for hours. Then we were given papers that said we were free to leave the court and go out on the streets, but had to leave South Africa within forty-eight hours. If we didn't leave, we'd be arrested and given big jail sentences.

I had only one plan: I would go to Johannesburg and declare myself as an asylum seeker. A Kenyan guy from the jail came with me. I bought a ticket and we got onto a train, which was the first time I'd been on one. I sat on the seat, my Kenyan friend hiding under my seat because he didn't have a ticket.

It was September, late winter in South Africa. The train went overnight and became cold, cold, cold. We arrived in Johannesburg about six o'clock in the morning, but disastrously for him, my Kenyan friend was caught without a ticket and arrested. I never found out what happened to him.

I walked outside the station. If I had been in big cities before, they were nothing compared to this. This city was too big, there were people *everywhere*. What could I do now? I didn't know. I found a street where there were lots of Senegalese and Nigerians doing business. I found a guy who was very black, and approached him, thinking he was from Sudan, but he was Senegalese. I asked him if he knew where the Sudanese were. He told me to go to Doornfontein, which apparently was a suburb in the centre of Johannesburg.

I kept walking, asking people the direction of Doornfontein. When I got there, I found a lot of Congolese and Burundians. I asked for Sudanese but there didn't seem to be any around. Some Burundian men bought me something to eat, and while I was with them I met a guy called Pombe, who asked me if I wanted to start a job the next day.

'What do you want me to do?' I asked.

'Can you sell sweets for me? You can come to my house and sleep and eat for free, plus I'll give you seven rand a day.'

It sounded like a great deal to me, at least while I applied for asylum. If I was going to stay beyond my forty-eight hours, I would need a job.

'Fine,' I said.

I slept in his house, and the next day he took me to work. Pombe had a little stall selling sweets, and on that first morning I sold three hundred rand worth of goods. He gave me seven. Towards the middle of the day I told him I wanted to go to the Department of Home Affairs to declare myself as an asylum seeker. Pombe said I could go. I don't know if he expected to see me again.

At the Department of Home Affairs they told me to go to the Jesuit Refugee Service office, where I would have to prove I was from Sudan.

At the JRS, an official sat me down for an interview.

'Where are you from?'

'Sudan.'

'Huh?' he said sceptically.

He brought out a map and asked me what was the capital city, who was the president, and which province did I come from?

After I answered his questions (correctly), and told him my story, he sent me back to the Department of Home Affairs, where they gave me a temporary permit which I would have to renew every three months. Getting the permit was a great relief, because in South Africa being without a permit meant that you could go to prison any day. I looked at this permit as the first step in my official freedom: at last I had a piece of paper certifying who I was, and shielding me, I hoped, from deportation, arbitrary arrest or bad treatment by police.

I lived and worked with Pombe for two months. I wanted to start my own business, but couldn't save anything on a wage of seven rand a day. I'd heard about another Sudanese guy doing business in Pretoria. His name was Gakwich. He'd come from Pretoria to buy stock, and when we met he asked me about my history. Now I called him, and he said he'd pay me one hundred and fifty rand a week working for him. It was a big pay rise on what I was getting from Pombe.

I went to a suburb of Pretoria called Garankuwa, where I found Gakwich living in a big house with three bedrooms and his own backyard. At Pombe's house I had been in one room sharing with seven men. Here I had a bedroom all to myself. It felt a little strange lying awake at night, listening for the sound of other people breathing. I had shared everything, beds and rooms, for my whole life. But I quickly got over the strangeness; after a week or so I began to relax with the idea that nobody was going to creep up and steal my things. Later, I would share the room with a Sudanese guy called James Tut. He had been living in Cape Town but was attacked there by some Sudanese Arabs. He had a big knife wound in his left arm. For some Sudanese, our troubles at home were impossible to escape; they followed us around Africa.

Gakwich showed me how the business worked. Near the Pretoria North Train Station he was selling umbrellas, Chinese-made shoes and second-hand clothes. He wanted to start a new business selling umbrellas on the train. He needed a salesman. It was the rainy season and there was a demand for umbrellas.

When I worked for Gakwich I would wake early, about five o'clock, and travel around on the trains. 'Umbrella, umbrella, umbrella!' I'd have two boxes on me with fifty umbrellas in each. Sometimes they'd all go and we'd make fifteen hundred rand before midday. Before long I was also selling toy telephones for kids, belts and other stuff. Gakwich was very happy with me for selling so much, and would race off to Johannesburg to buy more stock. I had no special gift for salesmanship or any other business skills, but I had an instinct for targeting the people who were ready to buy.

One morning I woke very early as usual, got onto the train, and was sitting in a carriage with my umbrellas. Two men came and sat next to me. One of them had given me a hand getting on the train. I said, 'Christmas is coming'; I was just making small talk because I knew they intended me harm. I said, 'Tomorrow, why don't you come to my house!' Maybe I thought they'd change their mind and not rob me today, rob me tomorrow instead.

The first man put his hand in my pocket. I grabbed his arm to stop him. The other man stood over me and said, 'You be quiet.' They spoke Zulu between themselves. Then the first man removed my wallet. I stood up to fight back, and suddenly there were seven of them holding me, with knives pushed against my body. They took everything I had, including my umbrellas. They got the train doors open and looked as though they were going to push me out. I grabbed the bar and pleaded with them not to. The carriage was full and the passengers all just sat there watching me being robbed.

Finally the leader said, 'No, we won't push him out.' As we slowed down for the next station they got the doors open while the train was moving, threw the umbrellas out onto the platform, and managed to jump out without falling over. They obviously knew what they were doing!

At Pretoria station I was worried about what I'd say to Gakwich. I talked to a few other vendors I knew, and soon James Tut came along. I was sitting there at the station, upset and confused and afraid.

'Cola, what happened?' James said. 'Why is your jacket torn?'

I told him I'd been robbed.

He'd already heard the story – people were talking about the guy who'd been mugged and had his umbrellas stolen.

We got a train home, and I told Gakwich the whole story. He didn't believe me. He accused me of making it all up so I could steal the umbrellas. I said he could keep my wages to replace the loss. I'd worked hard for that money, but I didn't want it if he didn't believe me. After his reaction, I didn't want to work for him any more anyway. 'Are you going to believe me when you find me dead?' I asked angrily.

So now I was unemployed. I decided to go with James Tut to Sister Louise, a Catholic sister working for the JRS in Pretoria. He said if I explained my situation the church would help me.

In the JRS office there was a man from Sierra Leone called Jing Thomas. He was a very intelligent guy who used to be a journalist in his home country. He talked to Sister Louise, came back to me and said she would help me – the JRS would give me two hundred and thirty rand a month to tide me over during my unemployment.

I wasn't going back to live with Gakwich, but I knew some other Sudanese boys in the Garankuwa area. One was called Williams and another was Malual Madut. I'd known both of them in the transit camp in Zimbabwe, and they had come to South Africa before me. They lived in a small house and were paying ninety rand a month in rent. They were also selling sweets but were only grossing about fifty rand a day. I said I'd pay the rent out of the money Sister Louise had given me.

Another man, also called William, came from Zimbabwe and we welcomed him to come and live with us.

I still wanted to start my own business. I was making more and more contacts around Pretoria with other African migrants. A Congolese guy called Geepepe said we could work together and he'd pay me commission instead of a wage. He traded in leather belts. He said, 'If I buy a belt for ten rand and you sell it for twenty rand, you take five and I take five of the profit. So if you work hard and advertise the business, the more you make. You could make two hundred and fifty or three hundred a day in commission!'

I said: 'That sounds good, brother.'

Geepepe specialised in belts, toy guns and toy cell phones. He'd give me a hundred belts which I put on my back, walking around the trains calling, 'Belts! Belts! Belts!' Sometimes I'd target children, going up to them with the plastic phones and playing their fake ring tones. The kids would cry and pester their mothers to buy these toys. If I did my job well, the mothers didn't have any option.

Before long, business was going really well. I'd come home having made two hundred rand in a day. Geepepe became my best friend, and we worked very well together.

At this time I also met my old friend, Benjamin Bol Bol, who had followed me from Zimbabwe. Together we pooled our money from the JRS to rent a house. Typical of my friends on this journey, Bol Bol had bobbed up in different countries: Kenya, Zimbabwe, now here. He came from the Bahr-el-Ghazal region in Sudan, west of Panaruu, and was a short, lightly built guy like me. In the SPLA, he had driven tanks. We always had a lot to talk about. He loved chess and was an extremely gifted soccer player – if there hadn't been a war in Sudan, who knows how far he might have gone?

For the first time in a long time, I felt that things were going my way. Finally I was in an affluent country where I would be free to work hard and make something of my life. The threat of being attacked or robbed, which had hung over me perpetually for so many years, seemed to have been lifted. Instead of just battling to stand still, I could move forward – or so I thought.

But I hadn't come on this long journey to spend the rest of my life coaxing mothers to buy pretend cell phones for their kids. Jing Thomas asked me what I really wanted to do. I told him I wanted to go to school. He said he knew a white man, a human rights lawyer called Jacob Van Garderen, who had helped another Sudanese guy get into school.

After an introduction from Jing, I went to Jacob's office in Pretoria. He asked what he could do for me. I said that life was hard for me in Johannesburg, and I wanted to go to Australia. I was keen to get in touch with my cousin Mayoum Mijok again, and to try to restart the resettlement application that had got lost in Zimbabwe.

Jacob said: 'If I give you a place to live, and a school, would you still want to go to Australia?'

I said I'd see if life improved. To be honest, I just needed some hope to hold onto. Jacob said he knew a priest who could accommodate me and send me to school. That priest was Father Dominic Baldwin, the man who would change my life more than any other.

I told Jacob: 'There's another young Sudanese guy called Bol Bol, a similar age as me. Can you help him too?'

He said: 'Cola, that would be a little bit hard.'

I said: 'If you helped me alone, I'd feel too bad. I'd rather suffer in the street with Bol Bol than go to school alone.'

So when Jacob told Father Dominic about me, he also said that I had a cousin. Father Dominic agreed to help both of us.

Jacob said he'd put us up at his house for one week before sending us to Father Dominic. Jacob's house was in a very good suburb in the hills of Pretoria near the university. He had views over the whole city and he drove a BMW. He was living with his new wife, Karin, and had a young Sudanese man called Peter Deng living there. Peter was a refugee too and had met Jacob through the JRS, and now Jacob had as good as adopted him. (When Jacob and Karin later had a son, Simon, Peter became his adoptive brother.) Peter could use a computer, and Jacob told us we could cook whatever we wanted. We started relaxing, and I was beginning to feel confident about life. From Garankuwa to one of the best houses in Pretoria – things were on the up! Jacob worked in human rights, and was a Christian who had been brought up to respect all people, but I think the main reason he helped people like Peter and me was simple: Jacob had a good heart. I have never worked out why some people have it and others don't, but I have been grateful with all my soul when my path has crossed with these fine human hearts.

Then a week later, we went to Springs in the east of Johannesburg, where Father Dominic lived. He was a Catholic priest and had a house for young boys. He was seventy-six years old. An elderly lady, our gogo (or grandmother), lived there as the house mama, and there was another woman, Mama Anna, who did the washing. She and Gogo Jane lived in two rooms out the back. The house was not part of the church, which was a kilometre away, but was owned by the Dominican Trust, which would sponsor children and young people from needy backgrounds to come and learn how to live independently. If you were a resident, you had an obligation to look after the house and do jobs in return for the right to stay there.

Father Dominic was a white South African who had been a priest all his adult life. His parents were South African and German, and he had studied for the priesthood in Tanzania. As an old man, he was still tall, with thinning white hair. He joked all the time and had smiling, kind green eyes. He said that as a young man he had received a vision of helping the poor, and he had devoted his life to that since the 1950s. Some of those he had lifted out of the gutter were now lawyers and doctors in South Africa, and this gave him the greatest pride

The main house had four bedrooms. Father Dominic lived in one, and I shared a room with my friend Emmanuel Hubbi. Bol Bol and another guy, Kabelo, shared the third bedroom, and a South African guy called Ryan lived in a small single room. He had finished school and was working as an undercover policeman, or so we believed. Even Father didn't know exactly what he did!

Father was an excellent cook, and he taught us how to make good meals. We cooked mashed potatoes, pies, all sorts of European food like steaks and sausages which took me a while to get used to. Holding a knife and fork, rather than eating with my fingers, was another new skill for me. But it was heavenly to get used to having a full belly. On Friday nights when school closed we'd cook a delicious dinner. On Saturday mornings we'd drink tea. In the evening we could buy chips, and different types of sausage. In the house we'd cook as a team. If you cooked you didn't have to wash the dishes. The house was always spotless, and the sheets were freshly laundered. We had total freedom, but everything had to be clean and tidy.

On Sunday mornings we'd go to church and pray. Then we'd have a big Sunday lunch that Father would have cooked. Every fortnight we had to take turns cutting the lawn. There was a set weekly routine of chores, activities and duties. We all helped willingly, both because we loved Father Dominic and knew that it was our obligation. I must also say that the routine of knowing what each day of the week would bring slowly transformed me from a boy who lived to survive the present day into someone who could make plans for the future. The security of knowing what the week would bring could give me not only the gift of a week, but of a life ahead.

I had been to church back in Sudan, but we believed in our ancestors more than a Christian God. I found it easy to go to church in Springs, even though Father never forced us to go. I liked it because it made him happy, not because I was becoming a serious Catholic. Sometimes I'd miss a day, though. Father would say: 'Cola, come to church.' I'd say: 'Father, I'll pray at home, can you pray for me at church?' He always said he did. He was pretty soft on us. But there were times when we lied about having been to church, and Father would test us by asking us what he'd said in his sermon. It was all done in good humour.

We attended Veritas Christian College, where I started in Year Seven with Benjamin Bol Bol. There were two hundred and ninety kids, boys and girls, at the school. Lots of them didn't know the first thing about Sudan. They'd say: 'Sweden?' I'd ask them: 'What's the biggest country in Africa?' They'd say: 'South Africa.' I'd say: 'No, Sudan.'

People were surprised to see someone as dark as we were. On the second day of school, a kid teased me about walking from

Sudan to South Africa. They all laughed, as if it was a joke. I didn't take it well. What did they know of suffering, of losing their family and home to war, of walking thousands of miles to find somewhere safe? How dare they laugh at me! I had walked a continent, and they, from their complacent safety, treated my suffering as a joke. I wanted to fight with the kid. Then I thought, who cares? They were young; they hadn't seen the things I'd seen. I couldn't help it if they saw a lot of the world as a joke.

The teachers were very kind to me, though. They took the teasing seriously and stood on my side. They said: 'If anybody says anything to you that you don't like, never ever fight. Come and report it.' That made me feel strong, as though I could trust them.

We were in the school, going well, until 2001 when I started having some trouble. It began when I told Father Dominic I wanted to contact my younger brother Thonager, who I believed was still in Sudan. I had been in touch with a cousin, Bol Tambul, who had settled in Canada. He knew a guy in Khartoum who said he knew where Thonager was.

Since I had left my village, I had never spoken to or heard of my little brother. I was desperate now to find out if he was in the army, or back in the village, or indeed anywhere. Now I knew about resettlement plans, I started to think that maybe I could get Thonager out of Sudan to Egypt, and then to South Africa with me, or maybe somewhere in the West.

Father let me use the telephone. I called Khartoum and the guy told me where Thonager had been living. I eventually got in touch with some people and asked if my brother was there. A man said: 'You're big enough to understand this. Your brother was killed one week ago. He was shot during the fighting.'

My voice shaking, my face screwed up in disbelief, I asked more questions. What fighting? Where had he been? This man told me that Thonager had been going to school in Khartoum for a while, but the government had been recruiting southerners into the army to go back down south. Fearing he would be conscripted, Thonager fled to Panrieng – where he was recruited by the SPLA. He had been shot in a skirmish with government troops. I would later discover that my other brother, Monyleck, had been with Thonager and had carried him from the battlefield to hospital, where he died.

I was gutted. I couldn't talk to anyone except Father Dominic. We prayed together, and the next day I didn't go to school. I went to church and prayed. I was devastated. All that was left of my family now was my father, me and Monyleck. I clung to the hope that my young sister Athien was still alive, but I hadn't heard any news of her in years. I couldn't stop thinking about Thonager, that little boy who'd cried too much to join the army. The last time I'd seen him he was about seven. I still imagined him that way. How could a boy that little be shot in fighting? I couldn't get over it.

I couldn't concentrate in school. I just wanted to go home. What was the point of going on here if my family was dying? Father Dominic kept encouraging me to study, but I just couldn't see the point.

Wishing to give me a new direction, Father Dominic moved me from Veritas to Johannesburg Central College, where I started studying music. I was in love with music – it was the only thing that gave me peace. I was learning how to play the piano, and listened to every kind of music I could get my hands on: hip-hop, blues, reggae, rock, even classical. I excluded nothing. If it made sense to me, I liked it. At the school I began to learn about how music is composed, and there were so many students with different tastes coming from different places, I was exposed to every type of music there is. It seemed to be the only cure for my sadness.

***

Every three months I still had to get my permit renewed. I still have a copy of the permit – I hate that thing. It has been stamped so many times that it's worn out. Every time I look at it I am reminded of how I had to keep going to be recertified, joining those long queues in that office. Aside from the tedium, it continually reminded me that I was not a permanent resident, only a visitor, in South Africa.

One day Benjamin Bol Bol and I were sitting on the kerb in front of Father Dominic's house when police detectives came up and asked to see our papers. Two of the police were white guys, two black. The black guys were unfriendly and said our documents were fake. I said: 'No, they're real.' One of them said: 'I'll fucking shoot you in the face, I'll fucking arrest you.' I got angry, stood up and said: 'Shoot me, go on, I don't care.' At that moment, it was true: I didn't care. The frustration was overwhelming, and then, so soon after I'd heard of Thonager's death, life had no great value to me. I'd tried so hard to stay alive, and to steer away from trouble, and here it was, following me around. Yes, let them shoot me.

Father Dominic ran outside and asked what was happening. As soon as he appeared, the police stood up straight and acted friendly. Father Dominic said we were from Sudan. They said, 'Yes, yes, okay, we know,' and drove away.

After that I became too nervous to go out on the street. I was teased at school by the black South Africans. They called me *makwere-kwere*, a nonsense term of abuse that I think meant 'foreigner' or 'animal'. They wanted to provoke my temper, calling me many insulting names, saying, 'You took our land, you're selling drugs, you're a thief.' I became frustrated and isolated. And I was devastated about Thonager. I was becoming an angry, argumentative young man.

***

I studied at the college for nine months before I heard about the resettlement program in Australia. I contacted Mayoum Mijok again and asked if he could send me another form. He said: 'Yes, but who's going to pay for your flight if they accept you?' He wasn't in a position to be responsible for me.

I told him: 'Don't worry, I'll take care of my ticket.'

When I'd left Sudan, the only country outside Africa that I knew about was America. It was America I wanted to get to. I'd tried to get into resettlement programs in Kenya. For me, it was never going to be as easy as it was for the famous Lost Boys, who were turned into celebrities in America. They should have been called the Lucky Boys, compared to me and the guys I knew! Everybody wanted to go to America. I'd discovered in the camps in Kenya and Uganda that I was never on the inside track for that, so I'd lost hope.

But since I'd made contact with Mayoum Mijok, I'd started thinking more and more of Australia. It seemed not too far away on the map, and I thought perhaps I could stow away on a boat across the Indian Ocean. When people asked me where I was going to move to next, I was now saying, 'Australia, Australia.' But when they asked how, I didn't say anything.

In South Africa I started hearing of Sudanese who'd undergone interviews for resettlement in Australia and even been taken there. I didn't believe it. I spoke to Mayoum again and he sent me another form. I thought – but didn't let myself get carried away with hope – that maybe I had an outside chance.

Father Dominic didn't really want me to leave, because the other boys and I were his family. He'd have liked us all to live with him in South Africa forever, but he wasn't going to stand in my way – more than that, he was going to support me if I really wanted to go.

I filled in the form without telling him, though. I didn't want him worrying about something that might turn out to be a mirage. Benjamin Bol Bol filled in a form too. He was asked for a medical check. I went to the Australian Embassy in Pretoria and put in the form at 10 am. At 3 pm that same day they asked me to come back the next day for an interview. I had the interview with a woman called Paula, and it only took about fifteen minutes. She had interviewed Lost Boys in Kakuma and had resettled them in Australia. She knew the environment I'd been in. She asked me why I hadn't got resettlement in Kenya, and how had I moved so far through Africa. Where was my family? Why had I left Sudan? I gave her a rough outline – but not the whole thing in detail! To be honest, I was scared of the interview. I didn't want to prolong it and jeopardise my chances by talking about the SPLA or some of the worst things I'd seen. I didn't want her to be afraid of me, or dislike me, or think I was a political person. I think instead she was touched by the extent of everything I'd been through, and I was still only a young man. At the end, she told me to go out and get a medical check.

Benjamin and I thought we'd better talk to Father now. At first he didn't believe us. A lot of people were leaving South Africa and it wasn't easy to get into Australia. We didn't even have passports.

We said: 'It's real.'

He said: 'Are you happy to go to Australia?'

'Yes,' I said. 'I can't handle South Africa any more.'

That was enough for him. He gave us the money for our medical checks. We had to wait for the approval for three months. Then we were free to go to Australia – if we had the money for our flights. Father went and booked our tickets and paid for them out of his own money.

Father had never given us money. This was such a big thing. Even now I am touched and grateful that he would do this for us. Normally he would buy what we needed – food, clothes – but not give us money except for a little pocket money. We had a lot of good times with him, and he introduced us to customs like eating with knives and forks rather than our hands. He told us to say thank you, which we weren't used to saying. In Dinka culture, you never say thank you for food, it looks suspicious. The cook would ask: 'Why are you thanking me for food?' In Dinka culture, if you do something good for me, I'll do something good for someone else. That is my way of showing gratitude. Father Dominic taught us Western manners. Sometimes it felt as though we were doing nothing but saying thank you. Eventually we got it, though. We had to do more than simply say 'thank you' to Father Dominic for all he had done for us. I hoped to express my gratitude the Dinka way, by passing his kindness on to other people. In that way I could honour the great debt I owed him, and the great man he was.

One reason we were so keen to go to Australia was that there would be more opportunities there to help our families back in Sudan. In South Africa we were being helped – we were the recipients. But we wanted to be the ones helping; we wanted to do something for our families.

Bol Bol and I were still close to Jacob. When we told him the news, he and his whole family – mother, brothers and sister, wife, two little sons – were very sad to hear that we were leaving. We'd been camping together, we'd lived in their house, we'd babysat their children, and in a way we were like their own sons.

It was a great wrench to say goodbye. Jacob held a party for us and brought in some fine musicians. We danced and laughed and talked about the things that had happened to us together. Once we'd been to a restaurant where they let Jacob in, because he was Afrikaner, but kept us out, because we were black. Jacob was so mad he vowed never to go there again. Once we took Simon, Jacob's son, out in the street and played with him in the park. Police stopped us, asking if we'd stolen a white kid. Even though Simon was calling our names, they phoned Jacob at home to check on us.

When it came time to say goodbye, we didn't want to let go of Jacob's hand. Benjamin and I felt as though we were farewelling our own family, and leaving him was as painful as having a part of ourselves torn out.

We were to leave on September 11, 2003. As excited as I was, I forgot about the significance of that date. Like most Sudanese, I knew that Osama bin Laden had been in Khartoum in the 1990s as an ally and benefactor of the government. We knew him as a Muslim enemy in our country before he was an international terrorist and the world's most wanted fugitive. Bin Laden had given the Sudanese government money, arms and training in the early 1990s, for its war against our Dinka people. Sometimes his al-Qaeda fighters were captured in the south of Sudan, and their identification would show that they had come from Afghanistan, or the Middle East, so we knew they were not government troops. When I'd heard about the attacks on America in September 2001, I thought: Now, he's not only fighting against the Dinka, he's fighting against everyone!

Even though I was excited to be starting a new life in Australia, I was dreading saying goodbye to Father Dominic. He didn't come to the airport. He was crying so much I even reconsidered going to Australia. Gogo Jane was crying as well. All the neighbours came out to see what the commotion was about. The little neighbouring children started crying as well when they saw how upset Father was.

Bol Bol and I also had tears in our eyes. We did not know if we would ever see Father again, and knew little about what was awaiting us in Australia. Would it be better, or would we be wishing we were back with Father Dominic? We didn't know.

I was going with Bol Bol. He was going to Adelaide because his sponsor was there. Mayoum Mijok was in Sydney, so that was where I was going. Father had paid four thousand rand for our tickets. He'd also given us five thousand rand as pocket money. I still can't quite believe how good he was to us, for so long, even helping us to leave him. I owe him more than I can say.

CHAPTER 11

Australia

WE FLEW QANTAS. I came with two bags Father Dominic had given me, filled with nothing but clothes.

I had flown in a helicopter before, in Sudan, but then we had been herded in like goats. What was my first impression of being in a commercial jetliner? I was excited because we had our own seats! In fact we had our own TV and flight attendants asking us what we wanted to eat! More importantly, though, I finally had official papers, so I could relax about crossing a border.

A flight attendant asked me if I wanted some Australian red wine. Remembering what Father had told us about good manners, I said, 'Thank you, let me try.' She brought one of those very small bottles. Bol had one and I had one – it was powerful, making me want to go straight to sleep. But I also wanted to watch every channel on the TV and listen to every channel on the music system. I slept for about two hours in total.

When we landed in Sydney, the immigration officials asked us where we came from. They thought we were from America because I had on my Nike cap and an earring, and wheeled my two nice new bags. We looked as though we were coming from America, not Africa. There were other Sudanese on our flight who'd come from Kakuma, the refugee camp in Kenya, and they thought we were from America too. At the airport in South Africa we had helped them with filling in their departure cards and even using the toilets (I had to show them how the flushing and the taps worked). On the flight, they'd thought they had to pay for their food and were worried that they didn't have any money. I went up to them and said, 'It's all free, even the alcohol.'

These Sudanese looked as though they'd come straight from the war. They were thin, their possessions were in maize sacks, they wore cheap nylon clothes, and they were carrying Sudanese handcrafts made out of animal skins, which were taken away from them by customs. Their bags were checked, and everything was taken aside. Meanwhile, Bol and I were allowed to go straight through. Our years in South Africa had served us well.

Now it was time to say goodbye to Bol, as he was catching his connecting flight to Adelaide. He got on the train to the domestic terminal, and we promised to keep in touch. I would have liked him to stay with me, as we had been through many trials together, but I had to be strong in this new land.

After he had gone, I waited and waited at the airport. I didn't know who was going to collect me. I was looking around, and could see faces everywhere, none of them familiar.

Eventually a man came up and said: 'Are you Chol?'

I said: 'Mayoum! Mayoum! My cousin!' I hadn't seen him since I was five years old.

Trying to calm me down, this guy said: 'No, I'm Moses, a friend of Mayoum.'

We drove into Sydney and the weather was beautiful. Moses had a nice car and put some hip-hop in the stereo – it was the new 50 Cent CD.

214

I said: 'Moses, this country looks good.'

'Yeah,' he said, 'but you've got to work for it.'

I didn't feel put off one bit. I could work like an ox. I was bursting with ideas and plans for what I was going to do. Moses kept looking at me and saying: 'This is not Africa, you've really got to work hard here.' I said: 'I'll do anything.'

We arrived at Mayoum's house in Lalor Park. He had come to Australia in 1998 with his wife and two children, and by now they'd had another three children. None of his children spoke Dinka – they were total Aussies.

When I got to the house, the kids and I had a lot of fun. They were saying I was different from everyone else who came. I said it was because I'd been living in South Africa and had been going to school.

Mayoum came home that night. We talked seriously. He asked me about the family and I told him how many people were dead. He brought out a picture of three gentlemen from his photo album. He told me that one of them was my father as a young man, another was my Uncle Sejin, and the third was my Uncle Mayar.

Mayoum asked me: 'So which one is your father?'

I pointed to him, and Mayoum laughed. I was pointing to the wrong one. I suppose it seemed funny at the time, but it also made me sad. I had not seen my father for sixteen years, more than half of my life, and I couldn't remember what he looked like.

Eventually I was tired and had to go to bed. I had a bedroom in Mayoum's house. It had a child's bed, one wardrobe and a little table. At that moment I felt very happy. My life had changed for good. Seeing those young kids speaking proper English, with all the freedom they had, I could see that this was my future. I was happy, but I was also in a hurry – I wanted to catch up and learn and do everything in one day.

***

Next day Mayoum's wife, Martha, took me to Centrelink and the Commonwealth Bank to get my affairs sorted out. Mayoum said he was going to take me to school to enrol. I didn't want to go back to school, not after South Africa where schooling had led to me being victimised. This time I wanted to earn money to help my family.

I asked Mayoum to let me work for a while first. He didn't agree, and wasn't happy with my choice. I was his guest, and I should have shown more respect and agreed with his decision. But because Father Dominic had paid for my ticket, I felt that I was free now, that I didn't owe my future to Mayoum.

I spoke to Bol on the phone, and he had some exciting news – my old friend Angelo Kuot was there in Adelaide!

When I spoke to Kuot, he said: 'Come to Adelaide, I'll help you get a job!'

Without a pause, I said, 'All right!' He helped me get a ticket, and after two weeks in Sydney I flew to Adelaide.

In South Africa I had had no briefing on how to do day-to-day things in Australia: how to find a flat, make a living, get transport, do the banking, and so on. Nobody told me about renting, working, or how the law operated. When I came here, it was Mayoum who taught me many of these things, but I learnt the practicalities of daily life through my friends. I didn't mind. In every country I have been in, this is always how it goes.

Kuot was living with a white lady called Kate, a volunteer who helped Sudanese boys get on their feet in Australia. She came to pick me up from Adelaide airport with a card saying CHOL. When I saw the card, I was so happy to see her. She took me to Prospect, a suburb in Adelaide, where her house was. Kuot had a low bed in his room and I slept there for a few hours. He was meant to be coming home from work at midnight. I looked at the pictures in his room and was laughing to see him.

When he got home at one o'clock, we chatted until daybreak. We had so many experiences to tell each other – quite a lot had happened between Uganda and Adelaide! We talked about friends we'd known in Uganda. Some were already dead, some had gone back to rejoin the SPLA in Sudan, and some had disappeared. Kuot asked how Australia compared with South Africa. I said they looked exactly the same, with freeways, BMWs (though not as many in Australia) and Mercedes, and McDonald's. The only thing about South Africa that showed you were in Africa was how many blacks were around. The physical environment, the land, was similar in both countries. Kuot said what a good place Australia was and how life was going to improve now.

Since we had become separated in Uganda, Kuot had lived in Kampala for three or four years before getting a chance through the United Nations to resettle in Australia. He came in 2002, a year before me. He now worked for a car-parts company in Adelaide, making parts for the Holden Monaro. I didn't even know what that was. He was also working part-time assembling airconditioners for another company.

It's very important for Sudanese to share with and help one another, to make a chain of assistance. But that chain can only work if there is trust. At least, having shared so many experiences, Kuot and I knew we had that trust. In Adelaide, Kuot, Bol and I were going to get a house together and make our new life.

I stayed with Kuot in Kate's house for two months. Kate taught us a lot: household budgeting, keeping our receipts, managing our lives. It was reassuring to find someone in Australia who would be as kind to us as Jacob and Father Dominic had been in South Africa. We found a house to rent in Mile End. The house was nice, very big and old. We each had our own bedroom with one toilet outside and one toilet inside the house, and two sitting rooms. There was a garden outside with lemon trees. When we saw it, we immediately decided we wanted to live there.

Kuot found a job for Bol in a company called Godfrey Office Equipment. Bol went to work in the morning, Kuot went in the afternoons, and I cooked for them both. Two weeks after Bol got his job, he went to his boss, John, and asked for a job for me. I went in and John's offsider, a woman called Marcia, said: 'Are you sure you want to work?' They thought I would run away after a week or two. Once I assured them I was serious, they said they would teach me how to be a spray painter. Bol was doing spot welding. Together we were making filing cabinets.

A week after I got the job, I got a phone call from a cousin in Sydney who said: 'Your father is in Nairobi and he wants to talk to you!' She gave me a number and I called him. The last time we had spoken, I was a child. He had not even known I was alive, let alone in Australia! Once he had recovered from this surprise, he started talking away about how cold Kenya was, and how he needed me to send him money so he could go back to his second wife and kids in Sudan. He knew about Thonager's death but was vague on details about my family. I didn't know how to feel, but I thought I should send him some money. 'Give me one week,' I said. 'No,' he said. 'One week is too long!'

My father was impatient about a lot of things. He couldn't understand why I was not already a doctor, or a pilot. In Dinka culture, once the decision is made that you are a doctor, you simply become one, and then you learn how to do it along the way. You inherit your position, or you are given it. My father couldn't understand that it doesn't work that way here in Australia; that you have to study for a long time, and pay money to the university, before you can qualify. I gave up trying to explain to him why I wasn't instantly rich.

Kuot and Bol were kind: they said they'd support me for two weeks so I could send my first cheque to my father. He was very happy. I said, 'Dad, buy some clothes for yourself and go to the barber shop and have your beard trimmed.' He said, 'All right.' Then I said I couldn't send all my money to him, so he'd have to wait a couple of months before I could send more. I was very happy to be able to help him – if I'd gone to school, as Mayoum had told me to, I wouldn't have been able to help Dad get back to Sudan and buy clothes for his wife and kids. But it would have been nicer if he hadn't been so totally interested in what I could do for him.

I worked at Godfrey as a spray painter, preparing those filing cabinets, until one day my spray gun exploded in my hand. It burned my right arm from the wrist almost up to the elbow. They gave me two weeks off, and then I came back. The factory got very hot, and Bol left after six months. I stayed working there; it was enough for me that the job was secure. They taught me to spot weld too.

Three months after I'd spoken to my father, a cousin in Khartoum called me to say that my brother Monyleck would be there soon and we might be able to talk. I was excited to hear from Monyleck because, unlike my father, he was still with my own family and would have news. I knew about my mother, sister Ajok and brother Thonager passing away, but didn't know anything else. When I called the number in Khartoum, Monyleck and I were pleased to hear each other's voice. But sometimes, the more you change, the more you stay the same! We started arguing straightaway. I was angry at him over Thonager's death.

'Millions of people have died in Sudan,' Monyleck said. 'It was not my fault!'

I said he could at least have advised Thonager not to join the army, but he would not admit to having done anything wrong.

Even after all these years I was still angry at him for pressing me into the army. I cut the call.

Afterwards my cousin called and scolded me: 'You're brothers, you shouldn't fight. Monyleck is worried about you. Call him back.'

In the end I did. 'Why do we have to fight?' Monyleck said. 'There's only me and you left now.'

I said: 'What do you mean? What about Athien?'

He said she'd passed away. She'd got sick and was taken to hospital, where she'd died. Once again, I was ripped apart. She was the baby of the family. But I didn't cry, not then. I wanted to find out from Monyleck what kind of girl she had grown into. After our mother had died, she had moved in with Monyleck's family, where I gathered that life had been hard for her. As a female relative moving in, she would have been treated more as a servant than a family member. Monyleck assured me that until Athien got sick she had been happy and beautiful and would probably have got married. By picturing the life she might have led, I was able to find some happiness.

Eventually I sent Monyleck seven hundred Australian dollars. He was overjoyed – it was the first time he'd had money in his life. It brought him closer to me, and since then we have talked a lot. Once we started talking about something from my childhood that I'd forgotten or buried. Back when I was around seven years old, there was one time when we were told the Arab militia were coming and everyone ran into the forest to hide. My dad and Monyleck were there, and all of a sudden, out of nowhere, my dad and mum started arguing. My blind old grandmother was there too. Then my dad started bashing my mum. She was crying, Thonager was crying, Athien was crying. Monyleck tried to stop the fight and my dad hit him too. This was while everyone was supposed to be hiding. Dad kept bashing, bashing, bashing, and all the other villagers started running away from us because we were making so much noise we would attract attention from the Arabs. I just stared at my father, wishing I had the power to stop him. But I couldn't. After it was over, my father took my grandmother and my step-mother, and they left to go to the city. They told Monyleck to look after his mother and brothers and sisters.

When we came back out, we heard that the Arabs had killed people in our village and it was not safe to return. Monyleck got us a lift to the city to follow our father. We got there before he did – he'd had to walk, while we were given a ride. It took him a week and he said this was punishment for his mistake. He'd suffered for seven days walking with his mother, he said; he'd made a terrible mistake and wanted to be forgiven. He had to sacrifice a goat for the ancestors to forgive him. We killed the goat and were together again, as a family.

Monyleck said that the fight had been over my stepmother being jealous of my mother and wanting to get rid of her. She had told lies about Mum, and that was what had caused Dad to hit her. He was surprised that I could remember the incident, for I had been so young at the time, but once he started talking it all came back to me. I still cry over some memories of my mother.

Monyleck and I had argued ever since I could remember. I resented his role in recruiting me into the SPLA, even though I knew he had no choice. He was always a combative boy. But this story about our mother reminded us that we were brothers, that we shared these memories and many more. All our brothers and sisters and our mother and grandmother had been killed, and we were all that was left. We had to stop fighting now.

The owner of Godfrey Office Equipment was very kind to us, but some of our friends in Adelaide were getting into trouble with the police, getting caught drinking and driving. Adelaide started to seem very small for us Sudanese. Even though we didn't want to be disturbed, there were always Sudanese in trouble coming to our house. They wanted to go to nightclubs and they weren't polite. I was always hoping to keep things respectful and to live the way our fathers had taught us, but these guys wanted to disrupt things. They wanted to come at all hours and lie around drinking, making a mess, not cleaning up after themselves. The way I live, if you want to pay me a visit, I'd like you to call beforehand. But these guys would just drop over and stay as long as they liked.

Bol began to grow defensive and always wanted to do his own thing. We started to have disagreements. Bol became unreliable and often let me down when I wanted to meet him or ask him to do something. To him, this was 'freedom'; to me it was bad manners. Kuot went to Melbourne, and I went back to Sydney. When I got there, Mayoum laughed about our earlier arguments. He thought I'd learnt my lesson and should have listened to him in the first place, and now I was crawling back to him for help.

I moved back into his house in Lalor Park and looked for a job. Soon I came across a company called Selecopedic through some Sudanese guys who worked there. One of them, James, had to go back to university in Tasmania and wanted me to take over his job.

Alex Llavero, the general manager, interviewed me. He asked me if I could do heavy lifting. He wanted to know if I could start right now. I said: 'Tomorrow?'

This was March 2005. I began assembling beds. My job was called hogring. I used a staple gun to fix the parts of the beds together. It's dangerous work, and once I clipped my middle finger, injuring it quite badly. I worked there full-time until

2007, and I still work there part-time, assembling mattresses two days a week.

Sometimes I have wondered if troubles follow me around the world. I am an optimist at heart. In the struggle that takes place inside me between hope and fear, hope usually wins. But things have not always been easy in Sydney, and one event in particular made me wonder again if I attracted a cloud of bad luck over me wherever I settled.

On 17 February 2006 I went with two Sudanese friends, Chillim and William, to the 50 Cent concert at Olympic Park. We heard there was an afterparty at the UN nightclub in Oxford Street, so we went there at around 11.30 pm. We got there early, before a lot of the other concertgoers, because William had a car. We paid a $35 cover charge and got our wrists stamped. After reading the promotional material for the party, we had the idea we could even meet 50 Cent and talk to him about hip hop. I'd been playing a lot of 50 Cent records. I hoped at least to get my photo taken with him.

The club was overcrowded and the promise was false. There were other rappers there, including 50 Cent's crew, G Unit, but we couldn't get anywhere near them. 50 Cent never came, and everyone was disappointed because we had paid the money believing we would see him. But it was still okay – we had a nice group of five Sudanese guys and five Sudanese girls. Because we had arrived early, we'd been able to get in.

Meanwhile outside, because of the crowding, there were a lot of problems between security guards and people wanting to get in. At around 2 am, our group was ready to go home. When we got outside, Williams Agar, Chillim and I waited for some of our friends who were still coming from inside the club. William went back to look for them, while Chillim and I waited on the other side of the road. A security guy walked straight to Chillim and hit him in the face – without any provocation at all! He just walked up and went *whack*. There were some other Africans standing around, and most ran away. I didn't know what was happening. These were the same security guards who had let me in, so I wasn't scared of them. Then the guard who had hit Chillim walked up and smacked me in the ear.

He swore at me: 'Fuck off, get out of here.'

Another security guard shouldered me in the chest and pushed me down. I landed hard on the ground, my neck and back whiplashing from the fall. I crawled around, in pain and in shock. Were they going to start kicking me? Was it all starting again?

The police were standing nearby watching all this. The security guys were much bigger than us. The police came up and prepared to apprehend me.

I said: 'Hang on, *they* assaulted *me*!'

Another witness, a white man, came up to talk to the police. They tried to push him away; they weren't interested.

Eventually an ambulance came and took me to hospital. The police charged the security guard but released him the next morning. A couple of months later we told our side of the story in the local court, and the police spoke too, but the witness didn't turn up. I was told he was an American actor who had flown home since that night. The security guard had a lawyer, but we had the police, the witness's written statement, and video camera evidence. Yet we lost the case. It was like Africa, I thought, where justice is turned upside-down.

Since I was assaulted, I don't have as much respect for the police as I used to. I am an Australian citizen now, so I have no reason to be afraid of them as I was in Africa. But I have learnt that the police cannot protect you, and if you get assaulted, as I was, they sometimes act like it's your problem. I lost a lot of faith – except in defence lawyers! The case taught me that if I'm in trouble, a good defence lawyer can always get me off the hook.

Ever since then, I have had problems with my back. I had to resign from my full-time job, and I can't stand up for long periods. It prevents me from doing a lot of things I want to do, and a lot of things I have to do. Australia was the last place I thought I would be injured and live in pain. But I cannot dwell on that. What is a bad back compared with the challenges I have survived?

Today music plays a large part in my life. When I was living in Adelaide I went to a club and saw a DJ called Samrai and another called DJ Kronic. Their DJing involved scratching, and I fell in love with this sound. You could manipulate the record to make a new sound. You weren't just playing, you were creating. The music on the record wasn't just something pre-packaged for me to sit down and accept: it was a raw material for me to convert into something else, something new that I invented on my own.

After I moved back to Sydney, I was out walking in Parramatta when I came across a hip-hop shop called Lopez Records. The owner was a well-known DJ, Victor Lopez. I asked if he could help me learn. He said I had to buy a turntable, the 1200 Technics which many DJs recommend because the needle doesn't stick; then he said he'd teach me and show me the tricks. I went and bought the turntable for nineteen hundred dollars and a needle for three hundred dollars. Vinyl albums cost up to forty dollars, and singles cost more than twenty-five dollars – it's a very expensive industry! But I bought the records from Victor, and he helped me learn how to DJ.

I'd seen how kids in African communities in Sydney were interested in DJing, but there weren't many African DJs who had the skills to put on good concerts. I thought I could help teach the kids to DJ. I started teaching friends informally and giving other boys a chance to DJ on my equipment.

That got me involved in voluntary work with the migrant centre in Blacktown. I'd go two days a week to Merrylands Youth Centre, helping kids record their music in a studio. We put on shows to let them perform and display their skills. We hope to do this at other youth centres in the south-western suburbs of Sydney. I'm not the greatest performer, but I am a good teacher.

The big obstacle is the cost of studio time, so I spent about seven thousand dollars setting up a home studio. I'd been setting aside one hundred dollars a week for a down payment, and was able to purchase equipment on lay-by. This is the benefit in Australia of not spending money on a car! To me, a car is no kind of investment. I wanted to use what money I had to learn more and invest in a future.

Now I have the studio set up, kids can make appointments and come to do some recording. There are a lot of talented Sudanese DJs out there who I'm helping to develop. I have some problems with my landlord, who gets complaints about the noise, and when the equipment breaks I have to replace it at great cost. Sometimes I come home from a shift at the mattress factory and there are kids waiting for me who want to work in the studio until one o'clock in the morning. I don't mind. I see it as a way of eliminating crime. They rap about their life stories, and if they're doing that they're not out on the street getting into trouble.

I have a rule: if they want to come to my studio, I don't want to see them hanging at the train station. If I see them there, they can't come to my studio any more. If they complain, I say that even their mothers have rules. Most of them, because they want to learn, and have talent, accept that. I also encourage them to find jobs.

Sometimes I think they're lucky. They spent time in refugee camps and didn't see the terrible things I saw in Africa. They didn't lose their family members and their villages. They're the same age as I am, and they come from the same place, but they have lived completely different lives from mine.

I didn't learn the alphabet until I was ten years old – most kids have learnt it from the age of four. When I think about education, I feel that everyone knows more than I do. It's the same for a lot of African kids. We started learning so late in life, when we go to school in Australia we are such a long way behind. It becomes stressful, to be behind in school when you are older than the other kids in your class, and this can lead to problems at home. So a lot of these kids move out, and get into trouble; what they need is direction. They have so much talent, whether it's sport or music or anything else, but they don't have structure in their lives. They have the stories, but with nowhere to tell them they get bored and go to the train station and do drugs and commit crimes, and down it goes from there. A community structure would help them develop their skills and live productive lives. My hope is to provide that structure, and to help them make the transition from talented kids into adults with careers.

Africans form a big community here, but they don't have a place to focus themselves as a group. The networking that naturally exists among us – we all talk on the phone all the time – doesn't have a physical place to go. Instead, the place to go is the train station, where people see us as forming a ghetto.

We need leadership and coordination so that we can turn these great young soccer players into Socceroos, these young basketballers into Boomers, these young musicians into big performers. If we don't organise ourselves and give ourselves this structure, the rest of Australia won't ever know what we have to offer.

Epilogue

As I write, in early 2008, I am sharing a two-bedroom apartment in western Sydney with Biar Deng, a Sudanese guy who has no close family here. Biar arrived here more recently than I did, and has been working and studying accounting while working. I have bought him textbooks, helped him with his study, and advised him on day-to-day problems. I have become something like his older brother, which is nice for me. Not so long ago I lost my little brother, and now I have a new one.

I also have a good friend here called Daniel Magot, whom I met in Ifo. He followed me to Zimbabwe, South Africa and Australia. He works at night as a money-counter for the security company, Armaguard.

It's with Biar and Daniel that I spend most of my free time. For a while after I was assaulted, I didn't want to go out in public. We spend a lot of time at home listening to music and watching DVDs or TV. I'm still as shy and quiet as I was in the village in Panaruu. It takes me a while to open up to new people.

Which brings me to the question I have been avoiding: do I have a girlfriend? Am I going to get married soon?

Once day Monyleck phoned me and a woman's voice answered. She asked him to leave a message. Monyleck believed I must have married a white girl. When we next spoke, he said, 'You've married a white girl and you haven't told us! You mustn't keep this a secret!'

I had not married a white girl. The voice of my 'wife' was the recorded voice of Telstra Home Messaging.

Following this, Monyleck and my father started hassling me about marriage. My father wants me to go home and get married the traditional way, to a girl he will arrange for me. Also, if I take a wife, our custom dictates that I must also take a wife for my younger brother Thonager, even though he is dead.

But I don't want a traditional Sudanese marriage. For a start, if I have two Sudanese wives, I don't think the Australian law will look upon it very kindly. More seriously, I want to work hard and be able to give my kids a stable life. I don't want my children to live the way we lived. My wife has to be happy, and there will be no beatings.

And I don't want my children sleeping with cattle.

Many Sudanese men in Australia go home to get married, but they are often afraid of bringing Sudanese wives back here. If I find a wife in Sudan and bring her back to Australia, what will she think? The change would be so overwhelming for a Dinka girl from the country, I don't know how she would react.

Bol Bol married a Japanese lady he met in Australia, and has a daughter with her. Kuot, like me, still waits for the right one. Most of my friends aren't married.

When I tell him that I don't believe in arranged marriages, my dad asks if I will marry a white girl. I say: 'I will if I find the right one.'

I am scared that once I commit to a girl, she will want a bigger house, a bigger car, more possessions. Most of the girls I have met are a lot more materialistic than I am. They don't understand what it is to have nothing. There has always been a gulf between me and the girls I have known, and I understand that this gulf has been created by my experience.

Which is all another way of saying I have not found the right one yet!

Whether or not I find a wife, my father is always asking me when I am coming back to Sudan. I always have the same answer: when I am ready.

I don't know what it will take for me to be ready, but I will know when it happens.

The political situation, at least, is making it easier for me to go back safely. The south and the north have held a power-sharing truce since 2005, and in the 2011 referendum we will decide whether or not to remain one country. Although I have no Internet connection at home, I stay in close contact with Sudanese news through the Internet service at my local library. When I first got onto the Internet in South Africa, at Jacob's house, the only site I ever went to was the BBC, to find out news about Sudan. Since then, the Internet has made communication a lot easier, and I have a MySpace page through which I make new friends. With my older Sudanese friends, we mainly communicate by mobile phone.

I have learnt how the Sudanese government has turned on the people of Darfur, in Sudan's west, killing hundreds of thousands. Darfur is getting a lot more attention now than the war in the south ever did. Before, when the south was fighting the government, the Darfurians never sympathised with us. They thought we were just creating trouble, when in fact we were struggling for our own survival. Being Muslim, the Darfurians supported the government. But now that they are under attack themselves, they realise that Khartoum has always had a wider campaign to take by force the resources of other regions. With us it was mainly agriculture, as well as oil and water, and with the Darfurians it is land and oil.

I am relieved that international attention has finally come to the genocide in Darfur. We in the south of Sudan can tell the world that genocide has happened in our country before.

Many SPLA leaders are now in high positions within the Sudanese government, and in the military. I will always have mixed feelings towards the SPLA. They took me from my family and they brutalised me in Ethiopia. But when I look at the overall impact of what they have done, I admire the SPLA. After all, they saved the Dinka from extinction. When John Garang, the founder of the resistance, died in a helicopter crash in 2005, a lot of people lost hope and thought we would be overrun again. But the agreement between the south and the north has held up, and the south has built up good institutions to achieve peace and self-government. My Dinka people have a better future now than when I was in Sudan. In a terrible way, the war pulled us out of our primitive life. Many Dinka have been able to get an education in the West, and they can now go back and give Sudan the benefits of that education. The SPLA's campaign has been long and bloody, but the modernisation and survival of the south owe a lot to the SPLA and its leaders.

I think a lot about the people in my life, those who have helped me, those who have saved me, and those who have been lost.

My father lives in Bentiu with my stepmother and their two children. In his seventies, he is still working in wildlife for the government.

Monyleck lives in Juba, the capital city of southern Sudan, with his wife and Mijok's wife. All up they have seven children. He's still in the army, the old SPLA arm that has merged with their former enemies from the government while we all wait for the referendum.

My cousin Thomas Wour Kuol moved to Canada in 2005. He was resettled from Ifo, in Kenya. He waited in Ifo for ten years. He works in Canada in a factory. After he got there he emailed me, and we have spoken on the telephone.

Angelo Kuot lives in Melbourne and is studying environmental science. He is in the Australian army reserve, where everyone is impressed by his ability to handle weapons. Kuot is my best friend in the world, and we speak every week on the phone.

Angelo's brother, Garang, is in Kampala, where I heard he is a pastor. For such a difficult guy, this is something Angelo and I have to see before we will believe it!

I heard that Father Leo, the cranky priest from Nimule, passed away.

Father Joseph and I fell out of contact in Zimbabwe. I have since heard that he has gone to Sudan to work in a church mission.

Father Dominic is still in South Africa. He is very old now, and I speak to him from time to time. He has cancer, but his house is still open to boys who have nowhere else to go. I would love to go there and see him once more. I have promised him that I will one day follow in his footsteps and open a house for boys.

Jacob is still living in Pretoria. Unfortunately he separated from his wife Karin, which made me very sad. He lives with his two kids and his adoptive Sudanese son Peter Deng.

Benjamin Bol Bol, who came to Australia with me, lives in Adelaide with his Japanese wife and their child. He is studying commerical law and accounting at the University of South Australia. We haven't been in regular contact, but I hope to see him this year.

My cousin Mayoum Mijok went back to Sudan in 2007 to see his family, whom he hadn't seen for many years. He is hoping to help them start a business and make the most of life in the new Sudan. His wife and children are waiting for him in Blacktown.

James Makur, who I knew in Zimbabwe, has gone back to Sudan where he is serving in the army.

Malual Madut has gone back to Sudan, but I don't know where he is at the moment.

I don't know the whereabouts of Matouh, Arop or Samuel, my housemates in Uganda.

Williams Agar, who was in Nairobi with me, has moved to Sydney with his Sudanese wife and two kids.

I love Australia and am a proud citizen. When I first came here nearly all the Sudanese I knew were supporters of John Howard. We were grateful to him because we had been let into Australia while he was prime minister. But this all changed in 2007, when the then immigration minister, Kevin Andrews, made some comments about Sudanese. Some Sudanese had got into a fight in Adelaide, and one of them, a teenager called Liep Gony, was bashed to death. Andrews said that Sudanese were naturally warlike people who had brought their violent ways to Australia. He said that the Government had cut down on African refugees because 'some groups don't seem to be settling and adjusting into the Australian way of life'. He meant us – but it emerged that Liep Gony's attackers were not African at all!

We couldn't believe a government minister would say such a prejudiced and incorrect thing, just to win votes. From then on, we all changed our minds and supported Labor in the 2007 election.

The truth is that relationships between Sudanese tribal groups get better the longer we are in Australia. The changes in southern Sudan, where our people are no longer pitted against one another, have helped. But more importantly, now I am in Australia, I am Australian first, Sudanese second, and not really Dinka at all. We don't see ourselves as Dinka, Nuer or Nubian. Our dream is to see a Sudanese kid play cricket for Australia.

We all live under the one law here: Australian law. Sudanese kids are mixing with Australian kids, Sudanese have Australian boyfriends and girlfriends, and everyone is getting mixed up, in a good way.

Andrews was only manipulating the fact that many Australians don't know much about where we have come from, or the lives we have lived. It's up to us to create more of a link, to let Australians know more about us. We should tell Australians what it was like for us back in Sudan. I think that when we do, Australians will respect us more. I hope this book can do something to help.

When I walk around and look at people in the streets of Sydney or Melbourne or Adelaide, I know that few of them have suffered in the way I have. I don't resent this. Suffering is always relative, and I can't judge the suffering of others. Someone worried about their finances in Australia can be suffering more deeply than someone who is homeless in Sudan. Sometimes I even feel sorry for Australians, because if you are in trouble here, the bills just pile up and pile up until you have no way out. At least in Sudan, once you are poor, you don't keep getting poorer.

The only time I feel resentment is when I see kids who take their lives for granted. They think their mum and dad will be there forever, they will always have a nice home and will always be looked after. I get mad when I see these kids who think they don't have to work to maintain this. Life is never so certain, and you must always be prepared to work your way out of whatever troubles fall on you.

When will I be ready to go home? I have so much more I want to do in Australia. I have never held snow or ice in my hands. Maybe one day I can go to Mount Kosciuzko. I didn't even go to the beach until Christmas 2007, when I went to Kiama on the NSW south coast.

I first went to a Sydney beach on 20 January 2008. It was an incredible day. I went with some friends to Maroubra and we lost one of our group, my housemate Biar Deng. We reported it to the lifesavers and police. Nobody had seen him, and it was terrible: we thought he had drowned. Helicopters came in and were searching for him.

I will never forget the kindness of the people at the beach. They came up and offered us comfort, food and coffee. Everyone, it seemed, wanted to help find our friend. But he was nowhere to be found.

We went home to western Sydney thinking he had drowned. We were terribly upset. We got home and opened the door . . . and I nearly fainted in surprise. He was lying there, asleep!

We screamed and laughed and woke him up to ask what had happened.

When Biar had become separated from us in Maroubra, he had asked a local woman for help. They looked around for us, but couldn't find us anywhere. So she had driven him all the way home, more than an hour from one side of Sydney to the other, from the coast to the western suburbs. Then she drove herself back again.

That is the country I am in now.